For Rae —

Enjoy!

Sheilah

Simply Irresistible

Easy, Elegant,
Fearless, Fussless, Cooking

301-299-5282

By SHEILAH KAUFMAN

Cover Photo by Lee Van Grack
With Thanks to Helene and Barry Mankowitz for the setting.

Library of Congress Control Number: 2003096202

ISBN # 09718334-1-9

Publication #9,281

Printed in the United States of America.

To create your own custom cookbook, contact:
G & R Publishing Company
507 Industrial Street
Waverly, IA 50677
800-383-1679
gandr@gandrpublishing.com
www.gandrpublishing.com

DEDICATION

This book is dedicated to my family: my daughter Debra, her husband TJ, my son Jeffrey, and my husband Barry. A special thank you to my special friends who have supported me during this effort, taste tested my recipes, and offered their comments and critiques.

This book would not have been possible without my husband, Barry, and his computer expertise and help with all the big and little things I hate to do when it comes to working on the computer.

In addition, a big "thank you" to all my wonderful friends who so graciously shared their terrific recipes with me.

INTRODUCTION

After years of teaching cooking all around the United States, I still find that many people are intimidated by cooking. The culprit could be intricate recipes, or a lack of confidence in experimenting with new dishes.

I love to eat and entertain, but I don't want to spend endless hours in the kitchen. Over the years, I have developed a new "culinary philosophy" that takes the fear and fuss out of cooking. Besides being easy and elegant, recipes have to be "fearless fussless", which means: not too hard, a short preparation time; the ability to be made ahead or frozen; don't make a big mess (to be cleaned up); and the finished product is great!

By selecting recipes that entail advanced preparation and require a minimum of last minute attention, you can feel like a guest at your own party. Cooking can be fun and carefree!

Perhaps my crepes aren't perfectly shaped circles, or maybe they have holes in them, but after they are filled, rolled, and covered with a good tasting sauce, who will know the difference? Unless you can enjoy yourself, and be free of stress, what fun is there is entertaining?

This book contains an international assortment of tempting recipes designed for easy entertaining and family dining. There are many useful "Hints" throughout the book, which will make your cooking easier, and your finished products taste better. I learned them the hard way! They seem so simple that you won't believe how much improvement there will be in your finished product! In addition, this book includes my favorite recipes, ones that I use over and over for entertaining, holidays, and special occasions. I hope they will become your favorites and part of your family's tastes and traditions.

All of these recipes have passed the ultimate test: they have been tried and approved by family, friends, and students across the country. This book will teach you that cooking is an enjoyable experience!

This is written as a kosher book. If you do not keep kosher, where the word pareve margarine appears, you can use butter. Where "pareve" appears it indicates a non-dairy substitute for butter, milk, cream, or whipping cream (so the recipes can be served with meat or poultry) you can use "the real thing."

ABOUT THE AUTHOR

Over the years, Sheilah Kaufman has earned a name for herself as a "chef extraordinaire" with her uniquely refreshing, creative yet practical approach that demystifies gourmet cooking. Sheilah's love of cooking and teaching reflects her feelings about friendship: "Entertaining is an act of friendship and generosity, accessible to everyone." Her recipes emphasis the practical, without sacrificing the demands of taste.

Under the banner of "Fearless Fussless" Sheilah has spent the past 34 years criss-crossing the country from Alaska and Hawaii to Maine, Florida, and Mexico, teaching her "fearless fussless, easy ways to elegant cooking" to all ages (including 2 - 5 year olds and their moms/dads!), lecturing and making personal appearances in department stores, gourmet shops, book stores, and trade shows. In addition, she does consulting and has developed recipes for international food companies, and has served as spokesperson for a number of international cookware companies. A frequent guest on major TV and radio shows, author of 24 cookbooks, she is also a contributing food editor to several local newspapers. Her articles on foods, book reviews, recipes, and Jewish holidays can be found on her websites:www. fspronet.com/sheilah/articles.html. She is a member of Les Dames D'Escoffier, and IACP.

GLAMOUR MAGAZINE says "if you like to entertain, "Sheilah's Fearless Fussless Cookbook" should be your best friend." "It doesn't matter if your crepes have holes in them, when filled, rolled, and covered with sauce, no one will know!" is a bit of Sheilah's advice which accounts for her effectiveness and audience appeal.

A native Washingtonian, she started life as an elementary school teacher. Since the age of 8 when her mother taught her how to bake (because she was a chocoholic), she has pursued her love of cooking and baking. By the time she reached college she was already selling her fabulous desserts. One day a group of women approached and asked her to teach them how to cook instead of continuing to pay for catering. After that she was off and running: teaching for Adult Education and the Recreation Department, traveling the country teaching in department stores and gourmet shops, and writing her books along the way. In addition she began making TV and radio appearances, and guest speaking/teaching appearances for organizations and groups.

Sheilah's newest books: SEPHARDIC/ISRAELI CUISINE and A TASTE OF TURKISH CUISINE (written with Nur Ilkin, wife of the former ambassador to Turkey) are now available.

Please visit my web site at www.cookingwithsheilah.com

IV

TABLE OF CONTENTS

Appetizers
& Soups

BRIE IN THE HOLE

This easy to do recipe is more elegant than just heating a Brie in the oven. *

5" wheel of Brie
1 to 2 Tablespoons Dijon or fruit
   flavored mustard

1/4 cup slivered almonds
1 round loaf of sourdough or flavored
   bread (like olive or sun-dried tomato bread)
   (bread must be bigger than the Brie in
   diameter)

Preheat oven to 350°F.
Cut a circle of rind from the top of the Brie leaving a 1" border.
Spread the mustard smoothly over the top of the exposed cheese.
Top the mustard with the slivered almonds.
Place the Brie on top of the bread, and cut a circle around it 2" wider than the cheese.
Remove the top of the bread and dig out enough bread chunks so the cheese fits evenly into the hole, with the top of the Brie even with the top of the bread.
Cut or tear the chunks and place on a serving dish.
Place the Brie in the oven and bake for 25 minutes, or until Brie is soft and runny.
Let guests spread the Brie on the bread (I love to spread the Garlic Paste first), also tearing pieces from the loaf. Crackers and party breads are also good to use.
Serves 8.

*A great variation is to remove the rind from the top of a pound Brie, place it on an ungreased cookie sheet, and spread the top with 2 Tablespoons of butter. Then sprinkle the top with 3 Tablespoons of dark brown sugar, topped with 3/4 cup chopped pecans. Broil 8" from the heat for 3 to 5 minutes or until bubbly.

HINT: To store Brie, wrap it in plastic or waxed paper and store in the "warmest" part of the refrigerator. If possible set it out 5 to 30 minutes before serving so it can come to room temperature.

"CRAB" WONTONS

1 pound cream cheese	freshly ground pepper
16 ounces fake "crab" or white fish cooked	pinch of garlic powder
1 teaspoon Worcestershire sauce	2 pounds won ton wrappers, room temperature
dash of Tabasco	oil for frying

In a large bowl, mix the cream cheese, "crab" (or fish after flaking), Worcestershire, Tabasco, pepper, and garlic powder. Mix well. To assemble the wontons, place a small amount of filling in the center of each wrapper. Fold the wrapper diagonally into a triangle. Dab a bit of the filling on the outside of the wonton on each side of the " mound" the filling inside makes.
Lift the corner of the triangle and bend it towards the dab of filling so the wide part sticks to the bit of filling along side the mound. Repeat with the other corner. What you now have what kind of resembles a frog. The top will be open.
Heat the oil in a deep fat fryer, deep fry pan, or wok, and when the oil is hot enough, drop in about 8 wontons at once. If they do not immediately rise to the top of the oil, the oil was not hot enough. Fry for a minute or two until wontons are golden brown, then drain well on paper towel. When wontons have cooled to room temperature, place in baggies and freeze. To reheat, preheat oven to 400°F and place frozen wontons on a cookie sheet and bake until hot.
Makes approximately 100 wontons.

CREAMY ARTICHOKE CROUSTADES

24 slices thin sandwich bread, crusts removed	1 teaspoons Worcestershire
4 tablespoons melted butter (approximately)	2 tablespoons grated Parmesan cheese
14 ounce can artichoke hearts, packed in water, drained well twice, minced	freshly ground pepper
	salt
1 cup mayonnaise	garnish: paprika
1 tablespoon Dijon	

Preheat oven to 375°F. Roll bread out with a rolling pin, until very thin and cut circles about 2 3/4" with a round cutter. Brush with melted butter and press each slice into a 1 3/4" diameter cup of a mini muffin pan. Press with your fingers so it fits snugly. Bake 5 to 10 minutes until lightly browned. Do not over-bake. Remove from pans and set aside on a baking sheet. Raise oven to 400°. Squeeze out any excess moisture from artichokes. Place in a large bowl with mayonnaise, mustard, Worchestershire, and cheese. Mix well, stir in salt and pepper to taste. Divide mixture evenly into croustades and sprinkle lightly with paprika. Bake 10 to 15 minutes, allow to cool slightly, and serve. Makes 24. May be frozen when cooled.

EGGPLANT SPREAD

1 large eggplant – about 1 1/2 pounds
8 ounces cream cheese
1 cup freshly grated Parmesan cheese

4 garlic cloves, minced
1/2 cup extra virgin olive oil

Preheat the oven to 375°F.
Lightly grease a baking sheet .
Halve the eggplant lengthwise and arrange, cut sides down, on prepared baking sheet.
Bake the eggplant in the middle of the oven until very soft, about 40 minutes.
Cool the eggplant until it can be handled, and scrape the flesh away from the skin.
Discard the skin, and place eggplant in the food processor.
Puree the eggplant with the cream cheese, Parmesan and garlic until smooth.
While the motor is running, slowly add the olive oil in a steady stream and blend well.
The eggplant can be made a day ahead, covered and refrigerated until ready to use.
Eggplant can be served by placing it on a leaf of lettuce, then sprinkled with pine nuts, tomatoes, artichoke hearts, etc. or serve with crackers or breads. Makes about 3 cups.

HINT: To eliminate the bitter taste from eggplant, soak the slices in salt water for 15 minutes, drain well, and then use in any given recipe.

GEFILTE FISH DIP

A new way to serve gefilte fish.

14 ounce jar any type gefilte fish,
   drained
1 Tablespoon or more white
   Horseradish
1 teaspoon lemon juice

freshly ground pepper
8 ounces cream cheese, softened
   to room temperature
1 to 2 teaspoons såt

In a bowl, mash the fish with a fork.
Add remaining ingredients and mix well.
This spread can be molded if the mold is first lined with plastic wrap.
Cover and refrigerate.
Serve with crackers or matzoh.
Serves 10.

GLORIOUS GARLIC LOAF

A favorite from my friend cookbook author Polly Clingerman.

1 pound loaf French bread
1/2 cup butter or margarine
6 garlic cloves, chopped fine
2 Tablespoons sesame seeds
1 1/2 cups sour cream
8 ounces Monterey Jack cheese, cubed

1/4 cup grated Parmesan cheese
1/3 cup chopped fresh parsley
2 teaspoons lemon pepper
14 ounce can artichoke hearts, drained
   and sliced
1 cup Cheddar cheese, shredded
6 ounce can pitted black olives - optional

Preheat oven to 350°F.
Slice the bread in half lengthwise.
Place bread on foil covered baking sheets.
Tear out large chunks of the soft insides of the bread, leaving the crusts intact.
In a large skillet, melt the butter and stir in the garlic and sesame seeds, stirring and cooking for a few minutes.
Stir in the bread chunks and cook until the bread is golden and butter has been absorbed.
Remove from heat.
In a large bowl combine the sour cream, Jack cheese, Parmesan, parsley, and lemon pepper. Stir in drained artichokes and toasted bread mixture, mixing well.
Spoon mixture into the halved bread crust shells and sprinkle with Cheddar cheese.
Bake for 30 minutes.
Drain the olives.
Remove the bread from the oven and arrange olives around edges if desired.
Slice and serve hot.
Serves 8.

HINT: Fresh garlic keeps until it turns soft, shrivels up or sends out green shoots. It is best stored whole, in bulbs, in a cool, dry place. Do not seal it in a container or store it in the refrigerator (since the flavor will diminish). If the garlic bulb is fresh, plump and firm when you buy it, it should stay fresh for up to 8 weeks.

GREEN OLIVE AND WALNUT SPREAD

Lila Barth brought this to an international gourmet luncheon ("cold foods for hot weather entertaining"). This can be made a day ahead, and stays in the refrigerator for a few days, or it freezes beautifully. Make a double batch!

1 cup pitted green olives
  (with or without pimento), chopped
1/2 cup fresh parsley, chopped
1 cup chopped walnuts
1/2 cup green onions, chopped

1/3 cup vegetable oil
3 Tablespoons lemon juice
1/2 teaspoon crushed red pepper
salt
fresh ground pepper to taste

Combine all ingredients except the salt and pepper in a food processor.
Process JUST until the spread holds together, and be careful not to puree!
Season with salt and pepper to taste.
Cover and refrigerate until serving.
Serve with crackers or bread.
Serves 8.

BEER CHEESE SPREAD

1/ 2 lb. aged Cheddar, finely grated*
1/ 2 lb. Swiss, finely grated
1 to 2 garlic cloves, minced

1/ 2 teaspoon dry mustard
1 teaspoon Worcestershire sauce
4 ounces ale, at room temperature

Place cheese in a processor or blender. Add remaining ingredients except for beer.
Mix well. Slowly add the beer, blending until the mixture is blended and of a spreading consistency. Store in a covered container, in refrigerator. Spread on bread, crackers, celery.
Serves 6.

Alternative is 3/ 4 lb. aged cheddar and 1/ 8 lb. Roquefort or blue cheese, crumbled and drop of Tabasco with other ingredients (6 oz beer, and 1 teaspoon grated onion or chives).

MANGO QUESADILLAS

These can be used for an appetizer or main course – just make sure you have enough! You can substitute papaya for mango or use both of them.

7 ounce jar roasted red peppers,
   drained
dash of hot sauce
4 (9 or 10") flour tortillas
4 Tablespoons (or more) pesto

1 large mango, peeled and chopped
2 cups grated Monterey Jack cheese with
   or without Jalapenos
about 2 Tablespoons butter or margarine

Preheat oven to 375°F.
Place the red peppers and the hot sauce in the processor and blend until smooth.
Place mixture in a small bowl. This can be done ahead, covered and refrigerated.
Place tortillas on a work surface and brush 1 TBL of pesto over half of each tortilla.
Sprinkle 1/4 of the cheese and mangos over the pesto.
Fold the other half of each tortilla over the cheese and mango, gently pressing.
Melt a tablespoon of the butter or margarine in a large skillet over medium heat.
Cook the quesadillas until golden brown on each side, adding more butter as needed.
Transfer quesadillas to a large baking sheet and brush the tops with the red pepper mixture.
Bake the quesadillas until the cheese melts and tortillas are crisp - about 5 to 10 minutes.
Cut each quesadilla into 6 wedges and serve with salsa and sour cream.
Serves 2 to 4.

HINT: One fourth pound of hard cheese (Cheddar, Swiss, Parmesan) will yield 1 cup of grated cheese.

VARIATION: SANDRA'S BRIE, PAPAYA AND ONION QUESADILLAS

1 tablespoon olive oil
1/2 large onion, thinly sliced
2 teaspoons seeded, minced jalapeno
4 large tortillas
8 oz. Brie, rind removed, diced

1/4 cup fresh cilantro, chopped
1/2 large papaya, peeled, seeded, chopped
sour cream
salsa

Preheat oven to 425°F.
Heat the oil in a small skillet over medium heat. Add the onions and jalapeno and sauté until the onion is very tender. Cool slightly. Arrange tortillas on a large baking sheet. Arrange Brie, then cilantro, papaya and onion over half of each tortilla. Fold tortilla in half and press to adhere. Bake until the cheese melts and the filling is heated through, about 8 minutes. Transfer quesadillas to plates and cut into wedges. Serve, passing sour cream and salsa on the side.

MUSHROOM CROUSTADES

2 Tablespoons butter or margarine, softened

24 slices soft, thinly sliced white bread, crusts removed

1/4 cup butter or margarine

3 Tablespoons finely chopped shallots

1/2 pound fresh mushrooms, wiped and chopped fine

2 Tablespoons flour

1 cup heavy cream, or substitute

salt

freshly ground pepper

pinch of cayenne pepper

1 Tablespoon finely chopped fresh parsley

1 1/2 Tablespoons finely chopped fresh chives

1/2 teaspoon lemon juice

3 Tablespoons fresh grated Parmesan cheese

additional butter or margarine for topping

Preheat oven to 400°F.

Spray or grease the insides of 24 three-inch muffin cups, (or 36 or more mini muffin cups) with the softened butter.

Cut each slice of bread with a 3" round cookie cutter (or smaller for mini tins), and carefully press bread into the greased tins, molding them into the tins so they form little cups.

Bake for 8 to10 minutes or until lightly browned. Remove croustades from oven (and their tins), and set aside for filling, or cool and freeze until needed.

Reduce oven to 350°F.

In a large skillet, melt the butter and sauté the shallots over medium heat, stirring for 3 minutes.

Stir in the mushrooms, cook and stir for about 15 minutes or until moisture has evaporated.

Remove skillet from the heat, whisk in the flour, blending well, then whisk in the cream and return the skillet to the heat. Bring the mixture to a boil, stirring constantly, and as the mixture thickens, turn the heat to low and cook another minute or two. Remove the pan from the heat, stir in the seasonings, herbs, and lemon juice and place the mixture in a bowl to cool.

The entire recipe may be made ahead to this point.

About 15 minutes before serving, fill the croustades with the mushroom filling, sprinkle the tops with Parmesan cheese and dot the tops with the additional butter.

Place the croustades on an ungreased cookie sheet and bake for 10 minutes. Serve immediately. Makes about 24.

HINT: Wash and store parsley in a tightly covered jar in the refrigerator. This will keep it fresh for a long time.

MUSHROOM SAUSAGE STRUDEL

4 Tablespoons margarine
1 medium onion, chopped
1 pound fresh mushrooms, chopped
salt
freshly ground pepper

1 pound raw sausage – as hot or mild as
  you like
1 pound box phyllo leaves at room temperature
1 cup melted margarine
1 cup fine unseasoned breadcrumbs

Preheat oven to 350°F.
In a large skillet over medium heat, melt 4 tablespoons margarine and sauté the chopped onion for 3 minutes. Stir in the chopped mushrooms, salt and pepper to taste, mixing well.
Cook for a minute and remove pan from the heat.
Mix in the raw sausage, stirring well.
Lay out the phyllo dough as directed on the package.
Grease or spray a large cookie sheet.
Brush the melted margarine on a sheet of phyllo and sprinkle it with breadcrumbs.
Place another sheet of phyllo over the first one, brush with margarine, and sprinkle with breadcrumbs.
Repeat this until you have done 5 layers.
Place the sausage mixture on top of the last layer and spread evenly over the phyllo.
Roll the phyllo the long way, like a jellyroll.
Brush the top and sides with the melted margarine.
Cut diagonal slits an inch apart and about 1/2" deep in the top of the roll.
Bake for 30 to 45 minutes.
If freezing, bake only for 15 to 20 minutes, cool to room temperature, wrap and freeze. To reheat, bake frozen on a cookie sheet at 400°F until hot.
Serves 10 to 12.

PAULA'S FABULOUS HOT JARLSBERG AND ONION DIP

4 cups shredded Jarlsberg cheese
2 medium onions, quartered and thinly sliced

2 cups mayonnaise, regular or light
dash of fresh nutmeg

Preheat oven to 350°F.
In a medium-size bowl, combine all ingredients, mixing well. Place in an ovenproof baking dish and bake for 25 to 30 minutes or until cheese is melted and golden. Serve with vegetables, French bread or crackers. Dip can be made early in the day and baked later. Serves 12 or more.

MUSHROOMS STUFFED WITH WALNUTS AND CHEESE

I first tasted these at a diplomatic party given by Nancy Marshall (who made these fabulous mushrooms). You won't be able to stop eating them.

48 small white button mushroom
  caps
olive oil (for brushing caps)
1/4 cup olive oil
1 Tablespoon sweet butter
1 cup finely chopped onion
1 garlic clove, finely minced
10 ounces frozen chopped spinach,
  defrosted, squeezed dry

3 ounces Feta cheese, crumbled
1 ounce Gruyere cheese, grated
3 ounces cream cheese
1 to 2 Tablespoons coarsely chopped
  walnuts
2 Tablespoons minced fresh dill
salt - optional
freshly ground pepper – optional
crushed red pepper – optional

Preheat oven to 375°F.
Remove stems from mushrooms, wipe with a damp paper towel to clean.
Brush tops of mushrooms lightly with oil.
Heat olive oil and butter in a small skillet and sauté the onions and garlic over medium heat.
Add spinach and cook 5 more minutes, mixing well. Remove skillet from heat and cool slightly.
Stir in cheeses, nuts, dill, and salt, pepper, and crushed red pepper to taste if using. Set aside.
Place mushroom caps round side down on a baking sheet and sprinkle with salt and freshly ground pepper.
Bake about 10 minutes. Turn the caps over and bake another 10 minutes.
minutes. Remove excess liquid.
Turn caps over and fill with spinach mixture.
Place baking dish in the upper third of the oven and bake for 10 minutes or until the filling is browned and the mushrooms are thoroughly heated through. Serve immediately.
Makes 48.

HINT: To keep cheese fresh, cover it with a cloth moistened in vinegar; or store grated cheese in a tightly covered jar in the refrigerator.

CARROTS WITH GARLIC AND YOGURT SPREAD/DIP

Carrots will never be the same after you've eaten this dish! Turkish zucchini can be used instead of the carrots, but a teaspoon of dried mint needs to be added to the dish. From *A Taste of Turkish Cuisine* (by Nur Ilkin and Sheilah Kaufman, Hippocrene Books).

4 cups plain yogurt   *or 1½ cups drained greek yogurt*
7 tablespoons extra-virgin
  olive oil
1 medium onion, finely chopped
1 pound carrots, peeled, coarsely
  grated

3 to 4 garlic cloves
1/2 teaspoon salt
2 teaspoons Aleppo pepper or paprika

Place yogurt in a colander lined with cheesecloth over a large bowl. Let sit and drain at room temperature for 4 to 5 hours. Discard whey/liquid. Set aside yogurt.

In a 3-quart pot, heat 5 tablespoons of the oil and sauté the onions, stirring over medium heat for 5 minutes. Do not let them brown or burn. Add the carrots, stirring to mix well, and continue cooking for 10 minutes. Remove from heat and let cool.

Crush the garlic and salt together into a paste in a mortar and pestle or chop them together with a knife, then using the flat blade of the knife grind them together into a paste (using circular motions of the blade). Place the cooled carrots in a large bowl and add the drained yogurt and the garlic mixture. Mix well and place in a serving dish.

Combine the remaining 2 tablespoons of olive oil and the paprika and drizzle in a design over the top of the carrots, decorate with olives if desired. Serve at room temperature or chilled. Serves 8.

HINT: When a recipe calls for Caramelized Onions, heat a pan on HIGH, add 1 teaspoon oil, heat oil, add 1 sliced onion. Stir and cook onions on high until liquid starts to cook off (the hot onions release their juices). Add some kosher salt to draw off the water. Add 1/ 2 teaspoon sugar. Stir well. When onions start to brown and moisture has evaporated, turn heat to medium. It is best to do more onions in a larger pan because there is more area to get rid of liquid, just keep on high heat longer. Stir often so onions don't get too done on the bottoms. Stir every 3 to 5 minutes.

HINT: To avoid a scorched pot when making yogurt or boiling milk: Wash the pot in water prior to use and DO NOT dry it.

PESTO CHEESE PARTY MOLD

I saved this recipe for 20 years before I got up the courage to make my own pesto figuring it would be very difficult. Was I wrong!

1 pound cream cheese,
  softened to room temperature
1 pound butter,
  softened to room temperature
2 1/2 cups fresh basil leaves
1 cup fresh grated Parmesan cheese

1/4 cup pine nuts
1/3 to 1/2 cup olive oil
additional pine nuts for garnish -
  optional

In a mixer, cream the cream cheese and butter until smooth, and set aside.
Chop the basil in a food processor and add all remaining ingredients (except cream cheese mixture), to make the pesto. Add oil slowly, and stop if mixture becomes too oily.
Mix until a paste is formed.
Drape an 18" square of cheesecloth into a 6 cup straight sided mold or flower pot.
Using 1/6th of the cream cheese mixture, pack it onto the bottom of the mold.
Top with 1/6th of the pesto.
Continue alternating and packing the cheese mixture and pesto until everything is used.
Be sure and end with the cream cheese mixture.
Cover the top with the sides of the cheesecloth and weigh down top with a can of something.
Refrigerate until serving and then unmold onto a serving platter.
Mold may be decorated by pressing additional pine nuts on top and sides before serving.
Serves 12 to 20.

PUMPKIN DIP

A wonderful treat for fall and winter and a sure winner at parties.

4 ounces cream cheese,
  softened to room temperature
3/4 cup (or more marshmallow cream)
cinnamon

3/4 cup pumpkin butter* (or canned pumpkin, increasing the amount of marshmallow cream and add confectioner's sugar)

In a blender or processor, combine the cream cheese, marshmallow cream, and pumpkin.
Place in a serving bowl and sprinkle with a tiny bit of cinnamon.
Cover and refrigerate until ready to use. It will keep for days.
Serve with sliced apples, pears, and/or gingersnap cookies.
Serves 8.

*The best pumpkin butter can be ordered from JMS Specialty Foods (Smuckers, Lost Acres) at 800/ 535-5437.

PUMPKIN EMPANADAS

This recipe is a favorite of Gail Belgard, who was one on my cooking students.

Dough *:

2 cups butter,
   softened to room temperature
12 ounces cream cheese,
   softened to room temperature

4 cups (or more) all-purpose flour

Filling:

16 ounce can mashed pumpkin
3/4 cup sugar

1/2 teaspoon nutmeg
1 teaspoon allspice

In a large bowl mix the butter and cream cheese with a wooden spoon or a fork.
Blend in the flour, knead for a few minutes and form into 4 balls and wrap each ball with plastic wrap and chill overnight.
Remove dough from the refrigerator 30 minutes prior to use.
Roll the dough, one ball at a time, on a lightly floured surface until it is 1/8" thick. Cut into 3" circles.
Preheat oven to 350°F.
Combine all filling ingredients and mix well.
Spoon a heaping tablespoon of filling into the center of each circle of dough.
Bring half the circle over the filling and press edges together, making a half moon shape.
Bake for about 15 minutes or until lightly browned.
These can be frozen and reheated as needed.
Makes 48.
*If desired, instead of making your own dough use a couple of packages of flaky biscuits. Just separate each biscuit into three pieces, and let sit on a lightly greased cookie sheet for 30 minutes, then fill and bake.

ROAST GARLIC SPREAD (PASTE)

I was surprised how many people had never experienced the pleasure of eating this healthy treat, nor did they know how to make it. Always good for unexpected company since most people usually have garlic and bread or crackers in the house.

as many garlic bulbs as you'd like to make – each bulbs serves about 2 or 3 people   .
a few drops of olive oil for each bulb
French bread or crackers
a warm Brie - optional

Preheat the oven to 400°F.
Lay the garlic bulbs on their sides and slice off the top 1/4" to 1/2" of each bulb, exposing the tops of the cloves. You should now have a flat top/surface on each garlic bulb.
Rub a drop of two of olive oil on the cut surface and smear it around.
Wrap each bulb in a 4"x 4" square of aluminum foil.
Bring the 4 corners together at the top of the bulb and twist to enclose the foil around the bulb.
Bake the garlic for an hour.
Garlic will be so soft (paste like) that it will spread easily.
I love to spread it on French bread and top it with warm runny Brie.
Serve with bread or crackers.

TEXAS "FUDGE"

The name refers to the fact that in Texas they use chilies (in everything) the way I use chocolate (whenever I can!). It tastes great hot, warm, or even cold, and freezes and reheat.

2 (4 ounce each) cans chopped
  green chilies, well drained *
1 pound Monterey Jack cheese, grated
1 pound Cheddar cheese, grated

6 large eggs, lightly beaten
5 ounce can evaporated milk

Preheat the oven to 350°F.
Pour the chilies into a 9"x 13" ovenproof pan, spreading the chilies over the bottom. *For Passover use fresh chopped green chilies or green peppers.
In a large bowl, combine the cheeses with the eggs and milk. Pour the cheese mixture over the chilies.
Bake for 40 minutes until lightly golden brown and firm to the touch.
Remove from oven and cool on a wire rack for 3 to 5 minutes before cutting into squares.
Serve hot or at room temperature. The taste changes with the temperatures!
Serves 12 to 15.

THREE CHEESE BOMBE

A most appealing appetizer to serve with French bread or crackers. It does double duty as a dessert after a hearty meal. Serve with a mixture of sliced apples, pears, grapes, and walnuts.

2 envelopes unflavored gelatin
1/2 cup cold water
1/2 cup boiling water
2/3 cup grated Swiss cheese

2/3 cup crumbled Bleu cheese
4 ounces Camembert cheese
4 large egg yolks
2 cups whipping cream

The day before serving, butter a 1 1/2 quart mold and chill it until needed.
Sprinkle the gelatin over the cold water in a small bowl.
Add the boiling water, stirring until dissolved.
In a processor using the plastic paddle, or using an electric mixer, beat the three cheeses until smooth.
Add the egg yolks, beat well, then add the dissolved gelatin and mix well.
In another bowl, at high speed, whip the cream until stiff. Be careful not to over beat it or it will turn to butter!
Using a rubber spatula, carefully fold the whipped cream into the cheese mixture and let it stand for 5 minutes before pouring it into the prepared mold.
Cover the mold and refrigerate overnight.
Just before serving, unmold the cheese bombe by setting the mold in warm water for 30 seconds and running a spatula or knife around the edges.
Turn out onto a large serving platter and garnish with fresh fruit if desired.
Serves 15 to 20.

Hint: Store Bleu Cheese in the refrigerator wrapped in waxed paper or plastic and away from regular cheeses. Serve it at room temperature.

CHEESE DELIGHT

Put it on bread, stuff it in mushrooms, tomatoes, or omelets. This is a great do ahead delight.

1/2 pound Gruyere cheese, grated
1/2 pound Swiss cheese, grated
1 tablespoon dry white sherry
1/4 cup plain yogurt
1 bunch minced green onions

2 minced garlic cloves
grated zest of one lemon
1/4 cup minced red onion
1/4 cup minced parsley

In a large bowl combine the cheeses, sherry, yogurt, green onion, garlic, and lemon zest. Mix well, cover and refrigerate for an hour, overnight, or up to two days. when ready to use, preheat broiler, and spread on bread slices, or stuff in mushrooms. Combine red onion and parsley in a small bowl and sprinkle on top. Broil until golden brown and bubbly.

TRADITIONAL QUICHE

Tarte au fromage, or quiche is one of the first French entrees that I learned to make. These open tarts are a classic French entree, and vary from region to region in France, although they originated in Lorraine. Originally from Italy, the fillings were baked in bread dough.

Pastry:

1 3/4 cups sifted flour	3 to 4 Tablespoons ice water
1/4 pound unsalted butter	pinch of salt

Filling:

1 / 2 pound freshly grated French	1/4 teaspoon salt
or Swiss Gruyere cheese	dash cayenne
3 large eggs	freshly grated nutmeg
1 1/2 cups whipping cream	freshly ground pepper
	1 Tablespoon butter

Prepare the pastry at least an hour before using.
Sift together the flour and salt, and cut the butter into pieces and scatter over the flour.
Using your fingertips or a food processor, work the butter into the flour until the mixture resembles cornmeal. Add the ice water gradually, adding just enough water to hold the dough together to form a rough ball. Wrap in waxed paper and chill for at least an hour.
Roll out dough on a lightly floured board, into a circle at least 1 1/2 to 2" inches larger than the diameter of the flan ring or tart pan you are using. If using a flan ring, place on a baking sheet
Place the dough into the pan and fold the excess along the rim, doubling the edge. Flute the edge all around, building it up to form the sides of the shell. Chill while preparing the filling.
Preheat oven to 400°F.
Beat the eggs until well blended, then add the cream and seasonings, and beat until well mixed. Add the grated cheese and stir well to mix evenly.
Pour into the unbaked pastry shell and dot the top with butter, and sprinkle with 2 TBL of cheese.
Bake for about 25 minutes of until the top is lightly browned and the filling is barely set.
Remove from the oven and let stand for a few minutes to cool slightly.
Serve hot, although it can also be eaten cold for lunch or picnics.
Serves 6.

TIROPITES

1 box phyllo, at room
  temperature
1/2 pound Muenster cheese, grated
12 ounces creamed cottage cheese
2 large eggs
1 small onion, grated

1 garlic clove, minced
2 Tablespoons finely chopped fresh parsley
salt
freshly ground pepper
1 cup (approximate) melted butter or margarine

Preheat oven to 400°F.
Unroll the phyllo and carefully cut it lengthwise into 3 equal portions.
Keep the phyllo you are not working with covered with a lightly dampened dishtowel.
In a bowl combine the cheeses, eggs, onion, garlic, parsley, salt and pepper.
Remove a strip of phyllo and place it vertically toward you on a flat surface and brush it with a
little melted butter.
Fold up about 2" of the phyllo from the bottom (making a reinforced place for the filling), brush
this flap with a little melted butter and place a tablespoon of filling on the bottom right-hand
corner of the phyllo.
Fold the corner over from right to left to form a triangle, then lift the corner on the left side
straight up. Now fold over from left to right. The corner is now on the right, so fold it straight
up.
Continue folding in this manner (this is how an American flag is folded) and lightly butter the
finished triangle.
Repeat this procedure with the remaining dough until all the filling is used up.
Place the triangles on an ungreased cookie sheets and bake for 15 to 20 minutes or
until they are golden brown. Serve hot.
The unbaked triangles can also be frozen. To heat, place the triangles directly from the freezer
onto a cookie sheet and bake in a preheated 400°F oven for 25 to 30 minutes or until heated
through.
Makes about 6 dozen.

YA YIA MARY'S SKORDALIA (Garlic Sauce)

In an age where everyone is worried about health and cholesterol, this is a healthy dip or spread for fish and all boiled vegetables.

1 to 2 bulbs of garlic, peeled
6 ounces walnuts
2 pound loaf white bread, crusts removed

1 teaspoon salt
3/4 cup extra virgin olive oil
3/4 cup red wine vinegar (or to taste)

Place the garlic and walnuts in the food processor and chop fine.
Place the bread in a large bowl, moisten/wet it and squeeze out all excess water.
Be careful not get bread so wet that it turns into paste.
Using an electric mixer, add the garlic and walnut mixture to the bread.
Begin to beat them together, adding the salt and slowly adding the oil, about 1/4 cup at a time.
When all the oil has been added, slowly start adding the vinegar, continuing to beat until you have a smooth, creamy consistency.
Keep in a tight container in the refrigerator. It keeps well for weeks.
Makes about 4 to 6 cups.

YOU'VE NEVER TASTED ANYTHING LIKE THIS GARLIC DIP

This will make a garlic lover out of anyone.

4 large cloves peeled garlic
whole bunch of fresh parsley,
   with long stems removed
6 ounce can smoked almonds

2 cups regular or low fat mayonnaise

This dip can be prepared a few days ahead of time.
In a food processor, carefully grind the garlic, parsley, and almonds until finely chopped.
Do not let the garlic turn to liquid!
Place in a bowl and fold in the mayonnaise. Blend well.
Cover and refrigerate. Stir well before serving.
Serve with fresh vegetables, crackers, bread, chips or whatever strikes your fancy.
Sometimes I spread this on grilled fish or chicken, or a potato and pop it into the broiler until the dip gets bubbly.
Makes about a cup and a half.
Serves 8, or more.

Hint: When fresh garlic and fresh parsley are chopped together, a chemical reaction takes place and the eater will not get garlic breath, or garlic upset.

SOUPS

BARLEY CHEESE SOUP

If you are looking to save calories, used reduced fat cheese products and low fat milk.
Barley is a good provider of protein and minerals.

1 1/2 cups chopped fresh
   or frozen broccoli
1/2 cup quick cooking barley
14 1/2 ounce can vegetable broth
1 medium carrot, peeled and shredded
1/4 cup thinly sliced scallions
2 1/2 cups milk

2 Tablespoons all purpose flour
1/2 teaspoon dry mustard
freshly ground pepper
3 ounce package cream cheese, cut into
   small cubes
1 cup shredded Cheddar cheese

In a large saucepan, combine the first 3 ingredients and bring to a boil.
Reduce heat, cove, and simmer for 10 minutes, then stir in carrot and scallions.
In a medium size bowl, whisk together the milk, flour, and seasonings.
Stir flour mixture into broth mixture and cook over medium heat until bubbly, stirring occasionally.
Cook for another minute.
Place the cream cheese cubes in a small bowl and stir in about 1/2 cup of the hot soup. Stir until well combined, then stir this mixture into the soup.
Stir in the Cheddar cheese until it is melted and serve soup at once.
Serves 4.

HINT: If you don't want to cry while chopping onions, light a candle (before slicing or chopping them) and place it near your cutting board. The heat from the flame burns off some of the noxious fumes and carries the rest away from your eyes and work space, taking the sting out of a normally tearful task. Other methods include refrigerating the onions first (chilling the sulfur oils reduces the volatility of the enzyme responsible for stinging the eyes), using a sharp knife, and slice the area around the root last (since this the area where most of the enzymes are).

BISQUE OF BUTTERNUT SQUASH WITH APPLE

This is a specialty of Paula Jacobson and has become her "signature" soup.

1 pound butternut squash,
   unpeeled, cut in half, and seeded
1 tart green apple, peeled,
   cored and coarsely chopped
1 medium onion, coarsely chopped
pinch of rosemary
pinch of marjoram
1 quart chicken stock or broth

1 slice Challah, trimmed and cubed
1 1/2 teaspoons salt
freshly ground pepper
2 large egg yolks
1/4 cup heavy cream or pareve cream
   substitute

In a large pot, combine the squash halves, apples, onion, herbs, stock, bread cubes, salt and pepper.
Bring soup to a boil, reduce heat and simmer, uncovered, for about 45 minutes, or until the
vegetables are soft.
Scoop the flesh out of the squash and discard the skins. Return the pulp to the soup.
In a blender or food processor, puree the soup until smooth....it may take 2 or 3 "loads".
Return the pureed soup to the pot.
In a small bowl, beat the egg yolks and cream together with a whisk.
Slowly whisk in a little of the hot soup beating constantly, then whisk the egg mixture back into
the pot of soup. Let the soup cook on low (do not let the soup boil), whisking, for a minute, then
serve immediately.
Serves 4.

CAROL'S AVOCADO GAZPACHO SOUP

1 large cucumber, peeled
   seeded, diced
1 large avocado, diced
1 large tomato diced
1 medium green bell pepper, diced
1 medium red bell pepper, diced
1 cup celery, diced
1/4 cup green onions, sliced
1/4 cup white wine

1/4 cup red wine vinegar
2 cups beef broth
4 cups crushed tomatoes
1 to 2 Tablespoons fresh chopped cilantro
1/2 teaspoon freshly ground pepper
salt
1 dash Tabasco
1 Tablespoon crushed garlic

In a large glass bowl, place all ingredients and mix together.
Cover and refrigerate overnight.
Serves 6.

HINT: Fresh tomatoes keep longer if stored with the stems down.

HELEN'S PUMPKIN LEEK SOUP

4 medium leeks, sliced
2 Tablespoons butter (or margarine)
2 cups peeled, diced potatoes
4 cups vegetable (or chicken) broth
3 cups milk (or milk substitute)
1 large onion, sliced
1/4 cup butter (or margarine)
16 ounce can pumpkin

1 bay leaf
1/2 teaspoon sugar
1/2 teaspoon curry powder
fresh grated nutmeg
3 Tablespoons fresh parsley sprigs
salt
freshly ground pepper

Prepare leek soup. In a large pot, melt 2 TBL butter (or margarine) and sauté the leeks for 3 to 5 minutes. Add the potatoes and vegetable (chicken) broth. Stir to mix well and simmer for 15 to 20 minutes or until potatoes are tender, stirring occasionally. Remove from heat.
Cool soup slightly then puree in a blender or food processor. Stir in 1 cup of milk (or milk substitute). Place in a large bowl and set aside.
In the same pot the leek soup was prepared in, melt the 1/4 cup butter (or margarine) and sauté the onions stirring until golden. Stir in the pumpkin, leek soup, and remaining ingredients except the remaining 2 cups of milk (or milk substitute). Mix well and simmer, stirring occasionally, for 20 minutes. Remove bay leaf and discard. Add milk, remove from heat, and let soup cool for a few minutes. Puree in food processor or blender (do not do this while soup is still hot). Return pureed soup to the pot, add salt and pepper to taste, adjust seasonings, and simmer for another 5 minutes, stirring often. Serves 6 to 8.

JONATHAN KRINN'S 2941 MUSHROOM SOUP

From at a fabulous restaurant in Virginia called 2941.

3 pounds of button mushrooms
2 Tablespoons of vegetable oil

1 medium Spanish onion, sliced thin
2 Tablespoons Kosher salt

Rise the mushrooms well in lots of cold water and drain. Place a soup pot on medium heat and add the oil. Add the onions and cook, stirring frequently, until the onions are fully softened, but still white (about 20 minutes). Add the mushrooms and the salt and continue to cook until the mushrooms are fully cooked, about another 25 minutes. Add enough water just to cover the mixture. Turn the heat to medium high and bring the mixture to a boil.
As soon as it boils, turn off the heat and let it cool for 20 minutes (this will make it easier to blend). Transfer the soup to a blender or processor (remove pusher/center of lid so any steam can get out), in batches and blend it until it is silky smooth (be careful and make sure you start the blender on low and then increase to medium high). Put the soup into another pot for serving. Season the soup with salt (if necessary) and black pepper. Heat and serve. Serves 4.

JALAPENO CHICKEN SOUP WITH SHIITAKE MATZOH BALLS

My family got invited to a "low fat, southwest style" Passover Seder at Jill Sullivan's, a well known Maryland cooking teacher. I immediately wanted to know what kind of food I would be eating and how "hot" or spicy it would be - it's not that I wanted to refuse an invitation to a Seder, I just wanted to be sure I could eat it when I got there! This was her low fat variation of chicken soup.

3 pounds chicken, skin removed
2 large onions, Vidalia if possible
1 to 3 Jalapenos, finely chopped
  with seeds removed
3 celery stalks, chopped into 1" pieces
3 large carrots, peeled and chopped into 1" pieces

1 bunch cilantro, chopped
3 cloves garlic, chopped
salt
freshly ground pepper
10 cups water or enough to cover chicken

In a large, heavy pot bring all the ingredients to a boil, cover, reduce heat to simmer, and cook for 1 1/2 hours. Strain the stock/soup and refrigerate until fat congeals on top. Skim off the fat. Serves 8.

MATZOH BALLS

2 ounces dried Shiitake mushrooms
2 to 3 cups hot water
1/3 cup vegetable oil
1 cup real egg substitute or
  2 eggs and 2 extra whites
2 Tablespoons fresh chives, minced,
  plus chives for garnish

1 1/2 Tablespoons chopped fresh tarragon
1 Tablespoon chopped fresh parsley
1 Jalapeno, minced with seeds
1 1/2 teaspoons salt
1/2 teaspoon cracked black pepper
1 cup unsalted matzoh meal

In a small bowl, pour hot water over mushrooms. Set aside to soak for 30 minutes. Once mushrooms are soft, chop half and thinly slice the remainder, discarding any tough stems. Reserve the mushroom water.
Combine oil, 1/4 cup mushroom water, chopped shiitakes, eggs, 2 TBL chives, tarragon, parsley, Jalapeno, salt and pepper. Mix , blend, stir in matzoh meal, cover and refrigerate for 3 hrs.
Heat the chicken soup to boiling with enough water to equal 14 cups (3 1/2 quarts) of stock.
With dampened hands, form cold matzoh meal into 1" balls and add to boiling broth. Cover and simmer until matzoh balls are tender and cooked through - about 40 minutes. Using a slotted spoon, transfer balls to a plate.
Add sliced mushrooms and the remainder of the mushroom water to the broth.
Return to boil then reduce heat to simmer.
Add matzoh balls and season soup to taste with salt and pepper.
To serve, ladle into bowls and garnish with chives.
Makes 8 to10 matzoh balls.

HINT: Any vegetable grown underground (potatoes, beets, carrots, etc.) should start cooking in cold water. Vegetables that grow above ground (corn, peas, beans) should start cooking in boiling water.

OLD WORLD LENTIL SOUP

Lentils, which come in brown, red, green or black, are a quick-cooking legume and pack a lot of protein. This is a full-bodied soup!

2 teaspoons salt
3 cups dry lentils
2 Tablespoons margarine
2 to 3 teaspoons minced garlic
1 medium onion, chopped
2 stalks celery, chopped
1 large carrot, peeled and chopped

freshly ground pepper
1 1/2 cups chopped tomatoes (fresh or canned)
2 Tablespoons dry red wine
2 Tablespoons lemon juice
1 1/2 Tablespoons brown sugar
1 Tablespoon red wine vinegar

In a large pot, bring 7 cups of water to boiling and add salt and lentils.
Cover and reduce heat to simmer, cooking over low heat.
Meanwhile, in a medium skillet, melt the margarine and add the garlic, onion, celery, and carrot.
Sauté over medium heat for 5 minutes.
Add mixture to the lentils and simmer over low heat until lentils are tender - about 35 minutes.
Add remaining ingredients and simmer for a few more minutes.
Serves 6 to 8.

REALLY BEST EVER CHICKEN SOUP

3 to 4 pounds chicken breasts or
   a large whole chicken cut up
1 large whole onion, peeled
6 carrots, peeled
3 ribs celery, with tops, cut into
   chunks

3 chicken bouillon cubes or 3
   Tablespoons packaged powder
3 Tablespoons fresh parsley
salt
freshly ground pepper

Place chicken in a large pot and cover with enough cold water to cover chicken, plus an inch more.
Bring to a boil, and as chicken cooks, skim off bubbles and "scum".
Add onion, carrots, celery, stir in bouillon cubes or powder and parsley.
Reduce heat to simmer, cover, and cook until chicken is done, about 45 minutes.
Remove chicken from pot and let soup cool. Strain the broth.
Keep chicken separate. Tear or cut into pieces and add to soup before serving.
Add salt and fresh ground pepper to taste.
May be made ahead or frozen.
Serves 6 to 8.

HINT: Fresh ground pepper has a lot more flavor than ground pepper. Once the pepper corn is crushed or ground it begins to loose flavor

ROASTED ONION AND SHALLOT SOUP

4 medium Vidalia onions, peeled and
   thickly sliced
12 large shallots, peeled and halved
   (or 16 small)
2 Tablespoons extra virgin olive oil
salt, to taste
1 teaspoon sugar, or to taste

2 teaspoons fresh thyme leaves
6 Tablespoons brown or white rice
4 cups vegetable broth (or stock)
2 cups chicken broth (or stock)
1/4 to 1/2 cup dry white sherry
1/2 to 3/4 cup (pareve) cream

Preheat oven to 400°F.

Place onions and shallots on a baking sheet. Sprinkle with olive oil; toss vegetables to coat lightly with oil. Sprinkle vegetables with salt, sugar and thyme leaves.

Roast, turning vegetables occasionally, for 45 to 50 minutes, or until lightly golden.

Place vegetables in a soup pot. Add rice, vegetable and chicken stocks. Cover pan and simmer 35 minutes. Using a blender or food processor, puree soup (this may have to be done in batches) and return to pot. Stir in sherry and cook 1 to 2 minutes. Add cream, mix well, heat through and serve. Serves 8.

SPARKLING STRAWBERRY WINE SOUP

This recipe is from a "pick your own strawberries" farm in upstate New York. Serve it before dinner or as a surprise ending for a special meal.

1 quart + 1/2 cup strawberries,
   divided
1 cup dry white wine, chilled
2 Tablespoons fresh orange juice

1/4 teaspoon fresh grated orange zest
   (peel)
1 cup club soda or seltzer, chilled
fresh mint leaves for garnish

Slice 1/2 cup of the strawberries and set aside.

Coarsely chop the remaining berries and place in the food processor. Puree until smooth.

Gradually, while the motor is running, add the wine, orange juice and zest.

Process until smooth.

Place mixture in a serving bowl, cover and refrigerate until serving.

Just before serving, stir in club soda and sliced berries.

To serve, spoon into wine or champagne glasses and garnish with mint leaves.
Serves 4 to 6.

CHILI CORN CHOWDER

According to my friend Sue Silver Cohen of Harrisburg, Pennsylvania: "This is the best ever soup… all the Cohen and Kogans love it…I like this chowder because its thickness comes from the potatoes and not from heavy cream…very easy to make."

1 large onion, peeled and sliced
1/4 cup Canola oil
3 cloves garlic, sliced
1 large red pepper, seeded and sliced
3 potatoes, unpeeled and sliced
4 cups chicken broth (or more)
1/2 teaspoon cumin

1/4 cup coarsely chopped fresh cilantro
kosher salt
freshly ground pepper
3 cups frozen yellow corn
8 ounces canned green chilies (mild), drained
1 small jalapeno pepper, seeded and sliced - optional

Pour oil in large soup pot over medium heat and sauté onions, garlic, red pepper, and potatoes until onion is wilted (about 5 to 7 min), stirring so all veggies sauté evenly.
Add broth and cumin. Continue to cook 10 minutes then add frozen corn, drained chilies, and jalapeno.
Continue cooking and stirring until potatoes are soft.
Add cilantro, salt and pepper to taste and heat through, about 5 minutes.
In batches, puree in blender or Cuisinart, so that soup is still a little chunky, not smooth.
If broth is too thick (this depends on size of potatoes you use), feel free to add as much additional broth as necessary, to your liking.
I usually make this soup a day ahead of time so flavors can blend. Re-heats easily.
Top with some chopped cilantro if you like.
Serves 6 to 8.

MANGO AND CARROT SOUP

This recipe is from my friend Barbara Wasser author of Divine Kosher Cuisine, which she adapted from an Asian cooking class she attended.

3 tablespoons canola oil
1 lb. carrots, peeled, sliced thin or chopped
1 large onion, chopped
1 1/2 oz fresh ginger root, peeled and grated
3 cups chicken broth (or mild vegetable broth)
15 oz can cream of coconut

1 large mango, peeled and chopped
dash hot sauce or chopped red chili
1 bunch scallions, sliced thin
zest of one lime, juice of lime
salt
freshly ground pepper
Garnish: 1/2 tablespoon chives, snipped
    or chopped fresh cilantro

In a large 4 or 5 quart pot, heat the oil and sauté the carrots, stirring, for 5 minutes, then add the onions and ginger. Mix well. Do not let burn or brown. Stir and cook until onion is translucent.
Add the broth and simmer 8 to 10 minutes, mixing well. Add the cream of coconut, mango, scallions, and chopped chili. Stir well and cook just until warm. Puree the vegetables and mango and return to the pot. Add the lime zest, lime juice, and salt and pepper to taste. Serve garnished with chives.
Serves 6 to 8.

Main Courses
(Poultry, Fish, Beef, Lamb & Veal)

POULTRY

BURMESE CHICKEN

Like most chicken dishes from Southeast Asia, this low fat dish is characterized by complex flavors.

1 pound eggplant, peeled and cut into
  1/2" slices
4 halves of boneless, skinless chicken
  breasts, cut into thin strips
1 garlic clove, minced
4 scallions, sliced
1 Tablespoons soy sauce

2 teaspoons chili powder
1 teaspoon turmeric
1 teaspoon ground ginger
1 Tablespoons cornstarch
1 cup de-fatted chicken broth
1 Tablespoon olive oil

Sprinkle the eggplant lightly with salt, and place on paper towels to absorb any moisture.
After 20 minutes, wipe eggplant with paper towel, and cut each slice into thin strips.
In large skillet, combine eggplant, chicken, and next 6 ingredients, stirring thoroughly to coat.
In a small bowl, blend the cornstarch and broth until smooth, then add to skillet along with oil.
Cover and bring to a boil, then reduced heat, cover and simmer 15 minutes, or until chicken and eggplant are tender. This can be served over rice.
Serves 4.

HINT: Tenderize chicken by rubbing the inside and outside with lemon juice before cooking.

CHICKEN CURRY

True Indian curries tend to be painfully hot, and don't contain the spice we know as curry powder. This modified version is an ideal company dish, providing an exotic flavor.

4 whole chicken breasts (bone in), skinned and split
7 Tablespoons margarine, divided
14 1/2 ounce can chicken broth
1 garlic clove, minced
1 medium onion, chopped fine
2 to 3 teaspoons curry powder
1 medium apple, peeled and chopped

1/4 cup all purpose flour
1/ 4 teaspoon ground cardamom
1 teaspoon ground ginger
1 teaspoon salt
freshly ground pepper
2 teaspoons lime zest
2 Tablespoons fresh lime juice
1/4 cup or more chopped chutney

In a large skillet, heat 4 Tablespoons margarine and brown chicken a few pieces at a time.
Return all chicken to skillet, and add chicken broth. Bring to a boil; reduce heat, cover and simmer 20 minutes, or until tender. Remove the chicken and keep warm.
Pour liquid in skillet into a 4-cup measure. Add enough water to measure 3 cups and set aside.
In same skillet, melt remaining margarine and add next 4 ingredients.
Sauté until onion is tender, about 5 minutes. Remove from heat, and stir in flour and spices.
Gradually stir in reserved liquid, lime peel, and juice, stir and bring to a boil.
Reduce heat, cover, and simmer 20 minutes then return chicken pieces to skillet, along with chutney. Heat gently just to boiling.
Serve over rice with these suggested accompaniments: shredded coconut, sliced bananas, chopped scallions, raisins, chopped hard-cooked eggs, and additional chutney.
Serves 6 to 8.

HINT: Add a little salt to the frying pan when frying to keep grease from splashing.

CHICKEN DIJON

An easy flavorful dish, that is good hot or cold. For Passover substitute matzoh meal.

3 to 4 chicken breasts (bone in), halved
1/4 cup vegetable oil (approximately)
cayenne pepper
1/2 cup Dijon mustard

1 cup fine unseasoned bread crumbs
 (made from fresh bread in processor or
 blender)
6 Tablespoons margarine, melted

Preheat oven to 350° F.
Clean chicken and pat dry. Place chicken skin side up in an ovenproof baking dish.
Brush chicken breasts lightly with oil, and sprinkle a little cayenne pepper on each piece.
Bake for 30 minutes. If using boneless breasts, cook only for 15 minutes or so.
Remove chicken from the oven and turn temperature to Broil.
Brush the tops of the chicken with Dijon mustard, brushing back and forth a couple of times. The more times you brush, the spicier the chicken will be.
Sprinkle the breadcrumbs over the mustard.
Drizzle each piece with melted margarine.
Broil for 3 to 5 minutes or until the coating is golden brown.
Serves 4 to 6.

CHICKEN NORMANDY STYLE

The modifier "Normandy" usually indicates that the recipe contains brandy or cognac.

1/2 cup margarine
3 pounds chicken, cut into 8 pieces
 (or use your favorite parts)
2 medium onions, peeled and thinly sliced
salt

freshly ground pepper
2 Tablespoons all purpose flour
1 1/2 teaspoons curry powder
 (or to taste)
1 cup pareve cream substitute
1/3 cup brandy

Melt the margarine in a large skillet over medium high heat, and when hot, add the chicken pieces, the onion, salt and pepper to taste.
Reduce the heat and cook the chicken, tightly covered for about 35 minutes or until it is fork tender and almost done. Then remove chicken to a plate and keep warm.
Combine the flour and curry and add this mixture to the butter/onion mixture in the skillet, stirring over low heat until smooth.
Stir in the cream substitute and the brandy and cook over low heat, stirring constantly until the sauce is thickened and smooth; then return the chicken to the pan and gently simmer for 10 minutes. Serve the chicken with the sauce over rice.
Serves 4.

CHICKEN PUTTANESCA

The capers, olives, anchovies and vinegar are all flavorful components of this full bodied, authentic Italian sauce (that is also low in fat). If you prepare it without the chicken it makes a satisfying meatless entrée. For Passover eliminate the pasta.

1 Tablespoon extra virgin olive oil
6 boneless chicken breast halves, trimmed of all fat
1 medium onion, chopped
2 Tablespoons minced garlic
2 (28 ounces each) cans concentrated crushed tomatoes
1/2 cup water
1/2 cup dry red wine

1/4 cup balsamic vinegar
3 Tablespoons chopped pitted green olives
1 Tablespoon capers, drained
6 anchovies, rinsed and finely chopped
salt
freshly ground pepper
1 pound linguine or penne pasta

Heat the oil in a large nonstick skillet over medium-high heat.
Cook chicken until lightly browned on both sides.
Remove chicken from the pan and set aside.
Reduce heat to medium and add the onion and garlic to the skillet.
Sauté until softened but not brown, about 5 minutes.
Add remaining ingredients except pasta and simmer uncovered, stirring frequently, until the sauce is thickened, about 15 minutes. Add salt and pepper to taste. Add chicken breasts, making sure to cover them with the sauce. Cover the pan and simmer until the chicken is cooked through.
Meanwhile, prepare the pasta according to package directions, then drain well.
Place pasta in a large bowl and toss with a little of the sauce to prevent sticking.
Place the chicken breasts on top, and pour the sauce over everything.
Serves 6.

HINT: To prevent crying over chopped onions put a little vinegar on your cutting board or light a candle before slicing or chopping them. Dr. Barry Swanson, a professor of food science, explains that the heat from the flame of the candle burns off some of the noxious fumes and carries the rest away from your work space, taking the sting out of a normally tearful task.

CHICKEN WITH MANGO

1/2 cup chopped fresh cilantro
2 1/2 Tablespoons finely minced fresh
  ginger
1/4 cup fresh lime juice
1/4 cup extra virgin olive oil
1/4 cup rum
1/4 cup dark brown sugar
1/4 cup lite soy sauce
2 teaspoons chili sauce

dash of hot sauce or a chopped Jalapeno
1 1/2 teaspoons freshly grated nutmeg
1/2 teaspoon ground allspice
1 teaspoon cinnamon
pinch of salt
4 whole chicken breasts, boned with skin
  on
2 to 3 cups chopped fresh mango for
  garnish

Preheat oven to 350°F (or heat up your grill).
Wash the chicken and pat dry with paper towels. Combine rest of ingredients except mango.
Take 2/3 of the sauce and pour over the chicken and marinate (for 15 to 60 minutes).
Place chicken in an ovenproof pan and bake, turning once and brushing the chicken with a little more of the sauce it marinated in. Chicken is done when there is no pink showing in the meat.
Spoon the remaining sauce (1/3 cup) over the chicken and top with the chopped mangoes.
Serves 4.

CHICKEN WITH PLUM SAUCE

Another great company dish that can be made ahead or frozen. I usually double the recipe to have an extra company meal in my freezer.

4 to 6 whole chicken breasts,
  (bone in), split in half
garlic powder
6 ounces frozen lemonade, undiluted
2/3 cup chili sauce
10 to 12 ounces plum jam or preserves

1 Tablespoon soy sauce
2 teaspoons Dijon mustard
1 teaspoon ground ginger
32 ounce can pitted plums,
  drained - optional

Preheat the oven to broil.
Place chicken pieces in a large ovenproof pan.
Season with garlic powder and brown under the broiler for about 8 to 10 minutes, or until brown.
In a large pot mix together the remaining ingredients.
Simmer, stirring occasionally for 10 to 15 minutes.
Reduce oven to 350°F and remove chicken.
Pour plum sauce over chicken and return to oven.
Bake for about 45 minutes, turning breasts once, and basting occasionally, until chicken is done.
Serves 6 to 8.

CHICKEN RATATOUILLE

2 chicken breasts, skinned, boned,
  and cut into 1" cubes
3 Tablespoons (or more) olive oil
1 zucchini, unpeeled, thinly sliced
1 small eggplant cut into 1" cubes
1 onion, thinly sliced or chopped
1 green pepper cut into 1" pieces
1/2 pound fresh mushrooms,
  wiped clean and sliced

16 ounce can whole tomatoes, cut up
8 ounce can tomato sauce - optional
3 garlic cloves, minced
1 1/2 teaspoons dried basil, crushed
1 Tablespoon fresh minced parsley
freshly ground pepper
any assortment or additional vegetables
  can be used

In a large skillet heat the oil and add the chicken. Sauté for about 4 minutes or until lightly browned. Remove chicken from the skillet and set aside.

Add a little more oil if needed and sauté vegetables for 5 to10 minutes, stirring occasionally until they are done the way you like them (crunchy or soft).

Add tomatoes and tomato sauce, if using, garlic, basil, parsley, and pepper.

Stir and cook for a minute or two and return chicken to the pan.

Cover and continue cooking another 5 to 10 minutes, stirring occasionally, until vegetables and chicken are tender and done. Serves 4.

CHICKEN REUBEN

7 whole sheets of phyllo
1/ 2 cup melted margarine
2 tablespoons or more spicy brown mustard
2 teaspoons caraway seeds
1 whole cooked chicken breast, cut into strips
  - low fat will work

salt
freshly ground pepper
1 cup fresh sauerkraut, well drained
4 to 5 Toffutti (white cheese like Swiss)
1/ 2 cup or more bottled 1000 Island Dressing

Preheat oven to 350°F.

Lightly spread 7 phyllo sheets with melted margarine and place one on top of another with long edge parallel to edge of your work surface. Spread top sheet with spicy brown mustard, and sprinkle with a teaspoon of caraway seeds. Place sliced chicken about 3" up from the long edge of the phyllo. Cover with the sauerkraut, top that with the dressing. Lay the slices of cheese over everything and sprinkle remaining caraway seeds if desired. Fold the 3" of phyllo over the top of the filling. Fold the sides over (like making an envelope) and roll the filling and phyllo carefully. Place seam side down on a baking sheet and brush lightly with melted margarine. Cut diagonal slits about 1/ 3 of the way through the rolled phyllo about 3 inches apart. Bake 15 to 20 minutes or until golden brown. Let sit a minutes, then slice through and serve. Serves 3 to 4.

COLD CHICKEN CHUTNEY SALAD

The lime zest is the secret ingredient in this fabulous dish.

1 cup mayonnaise
1/2 cup (or more) chopped mango chutney
  (or other flavored chutney)
1 teaspoon (or more) curry powder
grated zest of one lime
1/4 cup fresh lime juice
salt

4 cups cooked diced chicken breasts
  (about 2 pounds)
2 cans (14 ounces each) pineapple
  chunks, well drained
2 cups celery, sliced on the diagonal
1/2 cup finely chopped chives
1/2 cup slivered almonds, blanched and toasted

In a large bowl combine the mayonnaise, chutney, curry powder, lime zest, lime juice and salt. Mix well.
Stir in the remaining ingredients, mixing well until they are thoroughly combined with the mayonnaise mixture.
Cover and refrigerate the salad until serving. It may be made a day in advance.
Serves 4.

HINT: Grate the peels of citrus fruits (try not to get the inner white rind, which is bitter), place them in a tightly covered container, and store in the freezer and use as needed. This peel of these fruits is sometimes referred to as the zest and this is what imparts the citrus flavor to recipes.

FRENCH HERB CHICKEN SAUTÉ

2 whole chicken breasts, boned and cut in
  halves
salt
freshly ground pepper
4 Tablespoons (or more) margarine
1 cup dry white wine
4 large shallots, chopped

1 cup chicken stock or broth
2 Tablespoons all purpose flour
1 Tablespoon lemon juice
1 Tablespoon parsley, finely chopped
2 teaspoons dried chervil
2 teaspoons dried tarragon

Sprinkle chicken with salt and pepper. In a large skillet, heat the margarine and sauté the chicken until cooked and browned. Remove chicken from skillet and keep warm on a serving platter. Add wine and shallots to the pan juices and simmer until reduced to half the original quantity. Add the chicken stock and boil down until you have half the quantity of sauce. Melt 1 TBL margarine in a saucepan and blend in flour whisking to make a roux. Cook slowly over medium heat for 2 to 3 minutes until golden, then gradually stir in liquid sauce. Do not burn the roux. Stir in lemon juice and spices and simmer for a minute. Pour sauce over chicken and serve. Serves 4 to 6.

CHICKEN ENCHILADAS

4 cooked chicken breasts
1 teaspoon salt
2 Tablespoons margarine
1 medium onion, chopped
1 to 2 garlic cloves, chopped fine
4 ounce can chopped green chilies, well drained
16 ounce can tomatoes, with liquid
8 ounce can tomato sauce

1 teaspoon sugar
1 teaspoon ground cumin
1/ 2 teaspoon salt
1/ 2 teaspoon dried oregano
1/ 2 teaspoon dried basil
12 corn or flour tortillas
2 cups grated Soya Kass Monterey Jack Style
3/ 4 cup paerve sour cream, or plain soy yogurt

Preheat oven to 350°F. Slice chicken into thin slices.
In a medium saucepan, melt the margarine and sauté the onion and garlic until onion is golden.
Stir in the chilies, tomatoes, tomato sauce, sugar, and seasoning, reduce heat and simmer, covered, for 20 minutes. Remove from the heat. Remove any skin and bones from chicken and cut into strips
or pieces. Place a little of the tomato sauce in the bottom of an oven proof baking dish.
Place a few pieces of chicken in each tortilla along with some grated cheese. Fold tortilla in thirds and place seam side down in the baking dish. Don't worry if they split or crack.
Combine "sour cream" with remaining tomato sauce and pour over the rolled tortillas, making sure they are well covered. The dish may be assembled in advance to this point and refrigerated or frozen.
Sprinkle the remaining cheese on top and bake for 20 to 30 minutes. If baking directly from the freezer, increase baking time to one hour. Serves 6.

LEMON CHICKEN

My friend Pat thinks this is the best lemon chicken ever!

2 Tablespoons lite soy sauce
1/2 teaspoon sesame oil
2 Tablespoons gin or vodka
1 Tablespoon cold water
2 whole chicken breasts, skinned, boned
   and cut into bite size pieces
3/4 cup sugar
1/2 cup white vinegar
1 cup chicken broth
3 Tablespoons cornstarch dissolved in
   1/4 cup cold water
zest of 1 lemon
juice of 1 lemon

1" slice fresh ginger, grated
2 Tablespoons ketchup
vegetable oil for frying
3 egg whites, beaten slightly
1 cup cornstarch
1 carrot, cut in julienne strips
1/2 green pepper, cut in julienne strips
1 cup pineapple chunks, drained well
1/2 ounce pure lemon extract
lettuce or cabbage leaves

In a large bowl combine the soy sauce, sesame oil, gin, and cold water and add the chicken pieces, stirring to coat each piece. Let chicken sit in marinade for at least an hour.

Combine the sugar, vinegar, broth, cornstarch, zest and juice of the lemon, ginger, and ketchup in a heavy saucepan. Bring liquid to a slow boil, reduce heat and simmer, stirring constantly until thickened. Remove from heat, cover and keep the sauce warm until serving.

Heat a little oil in a wok or deep skillet.

Place the beaten egg whites in one shallow bowl and the cornstarch in another.

Drain the chicken and discard the marinade, then add the chicken to the frothy egg whites and stir well to coat each piece. Drop chicken into the cornstarch and toss.

Deep fry the chicken, a few pieces at a time, until it is thoroughly cooked. Remove from the oil and drain well on paper towels. Keep chicken warm.

Meanwhile, bring the sauce to a boil and stir in the carrots, green pepper, and pineapple chunks. Cook, stirring, for 2 minutes, then remove pan from the heat.

Stir in lemon extract.

Arrange a serving platter with lettuce or cabbage (whole or shredded) and spoon the cooked chicken over the lettuce, spoon the sauce over the meat, and serve with hot cooked rice.

Serves 6 to 8.

ORANGE GARLIC TURKEY BREAST

Janet Gaffney, a local cooking instructor shared a version of this (from Chile) with me in which the whole turkey is deboned and butterflied. I took this marvelous turkey recipe and prepared it the easy way! It has joined the list of favorite recipes that I now make for holidays. For Passover just omit the cornstarch, mix orange juice and gravy and cook the sauce until it reduces.

8 pound turkey breast

1/2 to 1/3 head of garlic, peeled and sliced

3 cups orange juice

kosher salt

3/4 cup fresh thyme sprigs

3 long stems of rosemary

3/4 cup fresh sage leaves

Orange Turkey Gravy:

juices from cooked turkey

1 or 2 cups chicken broth

1/2 cup orange juice

3 tablespoons cornstarch

The day before serving, clean the breast and with a small sharp paring knife separate the membrane that connects the skin to the meat on the upper part of the turkey (around the neck area) breast. Using your finger, carefully insert the slices of garlic, pushing them down and around the breast. Be careful not to make holes in the skin.

Place the breast skin-side up on large pieces of plastic wrap (big enough to enclose the turkey). Carefully pour 2 cups of orange juice (or using a baster) into the separated area between the skin and the meat. Bring up the pieces of plastic wrap and carefully wrap the breast so the orange juice cannot get out. Place in a pan and refrigerate overnight.

Preheat the oven to 500°F. Line a jelly roll pan with parchment paper or foil wrap and lay the turkey breast down and bake for 5 minutes to seal the meat.

Remove turkey breast from the oven, reduce the temperature to 350°F, and lightly oil a roasting pan. Scatter the herbs in the bottom of the pan and generously salt the breast all over. Place the breast on the herbs and pour any reserved extracted juices over the turkey (from marinating). Warm the remaining cup of orange juice and baste the breast every 15 minutes with orange juice and pan juices. Roast approximately 2 1/2 to 3 hours or until done.

Transfer the turkey to a serving platter and allow 15 minutes of standing time before slicing. Add 1 or 2 cups of chicken broth or stock into the remaining pan juices and strain and deglaze. Pour into a small pot and bring to a boil. Mix the cornstarch with 1/2 cup cold orange juice and whisk into the turkey gravy. Simmer and stir until thickened enough to coat a wooden spoon. Serves 8.

PAELLA

This national dish of Spain is a great one pot dish to serve to company. As close to the "real thing" as one can get.

6 pounds chicken, cut into serving
pieces
salt
1 /2 cup (approximately) olive oil
2 onions, finely chopped
1 to 2 garlic cloves, finely chopped
3 cups long grain raw rice
1 /2 pound salami cut into thin slices

2 ripe tomatoes, peeled and chopped
1 bay leaf
freshly ground pepper
pinch of saffron
6 cups boiling water
14 ounce can green peas, drained
14 ounce can green beans, drained
black and green pitted olives

Preheat oven to 325°F.
Wash and dry chicken pieces, season with salt.
Heat 1/4 cup olive oil in a large pan, and when hot, sauté chicken with onions and garlic until golden brown. Remove from pan and keep warm.
In the same pan, using more oil, heat the oil and stir in salami, tomatoes, bay leaf, salt and pepper.
Stir in the rice and saffron, and pour the boiling water over everything, stirring constantly. Return mixture to a boil and remove pan from the heat.
Pour mixture into a paella pan or large ovenproof au gratin or baking pan.
Arrange the cooked chicken and vegetables on top.
Place pan on the floor of the oven, or lowest rack if oven is electric.
Bake for 25 to 30 minutes or until all the liquid has been absorbed and the rice is tender. DO NOT stir after the pan goes into the oven.
When done, remove pan from oven, remove and discard bay leaf, and garnish with olives.
Serve immediately.
Serves 6.

HINT: Never refrigerate tomatoes, because they will loose their intense flavor and become mushy and mealy. Room temperature is the best way to store them.

QUICK CHINESE CHICKEN

There is only about 15 minutes preparation time in this recipe. Serve with rice or noodles for a quick dinner.

1 1/2 cups soy sauce
3 cups water
1 cup dark brown sugar

2 Tablespoons honey
1 Tablespoon dry sherry - optional
3 whole chicken breasts, skinned, boned
and cut into 1" pieces

In a large pot, over medium heat, combine all ingredients except chicken and cook for 10 minutes. Add chicken, reduce heat to simmer, and cook about 3 to 5 minutes or until pieces are done. Serves 6.

ROBERT ROTHSCHILD'S HONEY MUSTARD PRETZEL CHICKEN NUGGETS

This recipe works best if the chicken has been cut into small nuggets.

14 ounce jar Rothschild Raspberry Honey
Mustard Pretzel Dip , divided*
dash hot sauce – optional
1/2 teaspoon garlic powder
1 teaspoon freshly ground black pepper

1 1/2 pound skinless, boneless chicken breasts,
cut into 1" pieces
2 cups crushed pretzels (sourdough, regular, or
mixed)
1/2 cup margarine, melted

Combine 3/4 cup Pretzel Dip, hot sauce, garlic powder and pepper in a shallow bowl.
Whisk to mix well.
Preheat oven to 400°F.
Place the crushed pretzels in another shallow bowl.
Dip chicken pieces in mustard mixture.
Roll in crushed pretzels.
Place on a greased jelly roll pan.
Drizzle melted margarine over chicken.
Bake for 12 to 15 minutes or until chicken is done.
Serve with remaining Pretzel Dip.
Serves 15 as appetizers, 2 to 4 as a main course.

* This can be purchased directly from Robert Rothschild at 800/ 356-8933 if you can't find it at your local store.

RAZZLE-DAZZLE COCONUT CRUSTED CHICKEN WITH PINEAPPLE-APRICOT SALSA

Since you will want to eat this all year round, for Passover just substitute potato starch. This chicken freezes beautifully, and the salsa can be made ahead. This is from the fabulous ladies of Soirée catering.

1 1/2 pounds chicken tenders, or chicken cut into nugget size
1/3 cup cornstarch
3/4 teaspoon salt

1/2 teaspoon cayenne pepper
2 cups sweetened shredded coconut
3 large egg whites
canola, vegetable, peanut oil

Cut the chicken into bite size, nugget pieces. Mix cornstarch, salt, and cayenne in medium bowl. Place coconut in pie dish. Beat egg whites in another medium bowl until frothy. Dredge chicken in cornstarch mixture; shake off excess. Dip chicken into egg whites; then press chicken into coconut. Turn chicken over and press into coconut again to coat both sides.
Pour enough oil into heavy large pot to reach depth of 2"; heat to 350°F. Working in batches, add chicken to hot oil; deep-fry until cooked through, about 3 minutes. Using tongs or slotted spoon, transfer chicken to paper towels to drain. Arrange chicken on a platter. Serve with Pineapple-Apricot Salsa for dipping.

Pineapple-Apricot Salsa:

This wonderful salsa can be pureed and used for a salad dressing, or over fish.

1 cup finely chopped peeled cored fresh pineapple or cantaloupe or mango
1/2 cup finely chopped red onion
1/2 cup apricot preserves

1/4 cup chopped fresh cilantro
2 tablespoons fresh lime juice
1 1/2 tablespoons minced, seeded jalapeno chili

Toss all ingredients in small bowl to blend. Season with salt and pepper. Can be made one day ahead. Cover and chill.
Makes about 1 3/4 cups.

HINT: If you do not like to touch chilies (because of the heat in the seeds, ribs, and oil) put your hands in baggies to seed, chop, and handle them for a recipe. They freeze beautifully so fell free to chop extras or freeze whole chilies (and chop while frozen).

SWEET & SPICY CHICKEN WITH TROPICAL FRUITS

This low fat recipe is a sure winner. It not only makes a beautiful presentation but also tastes great...no one will believe it is low fat.

1 teaspoon vegetable oil
2 Tablespoons dark brown sugar
1/4 cup orange juice
1 pound boned, skinned chicken breasts,
   cut into cubes
4 Tablespoons (more or less) chopped
   Jalapenos
1" piece of ginger, peeled
2 Tablespoons vegetable oil
2 Tablespoons brown sugar
2 Tablespoons pink grapefruit juice, or
   any other tropical fruit juice
3 Tablespoons orange juice
1/2 teaspoon soy sauce

1 Tablespoon tamarind pulp concentrate or
   powder*
1 mango, peeled, pitted, and cubed
1/2 fresh pineapple, peeled and cubed
1 banana, peeled and cut into 1/2" diagonal slices
   (red bananas are preferred, if possible)
1/2 pink grapefruit, cut into small pieces
2 star fruits, sliced – optional
1/2 red bell pepper, diced
zest of one line
1/2 cup fresh basil leaves, thinly cut or chopped
1/2 cup mint leaves, chopped

Preheat broiler or grill.
To prepare marinade, mix together 1 teaspoon oil, 2 TBL brown sugar and 1/4 cup orange juice in a bowl.
Place chicken cubes in marinade and let sit about 30 minutes, or overnight in a plastic bag.
Thread chicken on skewers and broil or grill, basting each side.
Place the Jalapeno, ginger and remaining brown sugar in a food processor.
Slowly add in remaining oil, and process until minced.
Add citrus juices, soy, and tamarind, and process for 15 seconds until well blended.
Set aside sauce.
Place all fruits and bell pepper in a bowl. Add cooked chicken, lime zest, basil and mint.
Drizzle with sauce and gently toss everything to coat.
Serves 6 to 8.

*To prepare your own tamarind paste, put the tamarind pods in a large pot and cover with water plus an extra inch. Bring to a boil, reduce heat to simmer and cook over medium heat for 30 minutes, adding more water if needed. Place a colander over a large bowl and mash or push the tamarind through, crushing the pods and getting as much liquid out as possible. If needed, more boiling water can be poured over the pods and mashed to extract more liquid. Place strained liquid in a clean, dry jar, cover and place in a cool dark place.

SURE SUCCESS MOIST TURKEY

This recipe is for people who are tired of dry, tasteless turkey. It will be a favorite any time of year. For Passover, just switch to matzoh instead of crackers.

20 to 23 pound turkey, cleaned, with
   bag and neck removed from the inside
5 Tablespoons paprika
3 Tablespoons salt
3 Tablespoons pepper
3 Tablespoons garlic powder
1 Tablespoon poultry seasoning
1 cup white wine
1 cup cold water

1 stick melted margarine
1 pound salted crackers (like Ritz) or
   matzoh, broken into pieces, not crumbs
1 to 1 1/2 pounds fresh mushrooms,
   wiped clean and sliced
2 large onions, chopped
1 bunch celery, chopped
4 carrots
margarine for sautéing

The day before cooking, combine the paprika, salt, pepper, garlic powder, and poultry seasoning in a bowl with enough hot water to make "mud."
Rub mixture on the inside and outside of the turkey, and in both cavities.
Cover with foil and refrigerate overnight.
Preheat oven to 350°F.
Prepare basting liquid by melting the margarine, and mixing it together with the wine and water. Set aside.
In a large skillet, melt some margarine and sauté the onions and celery, and place in a very large bowl with the crushed crackers or matzoh.
Melt more margarine as needed, and sauté the mushrooms. Then add to the stuffing mixture.
Peel the carrots into the stuffing mixture and mix well.
Stuff both cavities of the turkey with the stuffing.
Place turkey in roasting pan, pour the basting over the turkey and make a tent cover with 2 pieces of aluminum foil.
Bake according to the cooking chart on the turkey wrapper. A 20 pound stuffed turkey takes about 5 to 6 hours.

HINT: All red spices (chili powder, paprika, red pepper flakes) and Tabasco should be kept in the refrigerator to avoid weevils and to stay fresher.

TOMATO SAGE CHICKEN

A delightful main course with a fat free sauce.

3 to 4 boneless chicken breasts, halved
1 cup chicken broth
1 large onion, thinly sliced
3 garlic cloves, minced
1 Tablespoon white wine vinegar
2 (16 ounce each) cans concentrated
  crushed tomatoes

2 Tablespoons balsamic vinegar
2 Tablespoons fresh sage leaves or
2 teaspoons dried sage
salt
freshly ground pepper

Cut each chicken breast half into 3 pieces and set aside. In a large skillet, gently heat the chicken broth and stir in the onion, garlic, and white wine vinegar. Simmer on low until the onion is softened, stirring occasionally. Add the chicken pieces and continue to simmer for 5 to 10 minutes or until the chicken is golden on all sides. Add the tomatoes, vinegar, and sage, cover and simmer over medium heat for 30 minutes, stirring occasionally. Uncover and simmer 5 minutes longer or until sauce thickens. Season with salt and pepper to taste. Serves 4 to 6.

HINT: Do not store herbs and spices near heat or light as they will loose their flavor quicker.

TURKEY BREAST ORIENTAL

This fabulous recipe is from *A GARDEN OF EATIN'* (cookbook) done by BSBI Sisterhood of Charleston, South Carolina. It is a real winner, and will become an instant favorite.

4 to 5 lb. whole turkey breast
3 cloves garlic, minced
5 to 6 Tablespoons soy sauce

3 Tablespoons red horseradish
1/4 cup apricot preserves
1/2 cup (Chinese) duck sauce

Rub the breast with the minced garlic, and place in a roasting pan. Combine the remaining ingredients and spread over the entire breast, inside and out. Cover and marinate overnight, turning the breast and spooning the sauce over it several times. Preheat the oven to 325°F and cook the breast covered with foil, allowing 20 to 25 minutes per pound. Turn to bake on each side. Uncover towards the end of the baking time to allow breast to brown. Remove from oven when juices run clear when pierced with a fork (170 to 180°F internal temperature on a meat thermometer). Don't leave breast in the oven too long as the internal heat will extend cooking process. Let cool about 10 minutes before slicing. If it looks like the sauce is drying out, add a little wine to thin it down. Serves 6. .

TURKEY BALLS IN HOISIN SAUCE

Great as a main course or as an appetizer. A friend gave me this recipe, and knowing I usually don't like "meatballs" raved about these. She was right, they are great!

1 pound ground turkey
1 Tablespoon plus 2 teaspoons soy sauce
1 large egg
2 Tablespoons plus 1 teaspoon dry
  white sherry – optional
1/4 cup bread crumbs
2 scallions, chopped

1/3 cup chopped raw cashews
9 ounces Hoisin sauce
1 cup apple juice
1 Tablespoon sesame oil
1 teaspoon grated fresh ginger

In a large bowl combine the turkey, 2 teaspoons soy, egg, 1 teaspoon sherry if desired, bread crumbs, scallions, 3 ounces Hoisin sauce, and cashews. Mix well.
Using your hands, make "meatballs" the size of walnuts and set aside.
In a large pot, bring the remaining Hoisin sauce, apple juice, sesame oil, 2 Tablespoons of sherry, and grated ginger to a boil.
Reduce heat to simmer and place the "meatballs" in the sauce and simmer for approximately 20 minutes or until browned and sauce begins to thicken. Serve with rice as a main course.
Serves 4.

FISH

BAKED SOLE

1/4 teaspoon salt
freshly ground pepper
1/8 teaspoon ground mace
1/4 teaspoon dried thyme
2 pounds sole fillets
1/2 cup dry vermouth
2 1/2 Tablespoons lemon juice

3 Tablespoons melted butter or margarine
3 Tablespoons melted butter or margarine for
  sautéing
1/2 pound fresh mushrooms, wiped clean and
  sliced
1/4 cup finely chopped onion
2 Tablespoons chopped parsley

Preheat oven to 350°F.
In a small bowl combine the salt, pepper, mace and thyme. Dust both sides of the fish with this mixture and place in a lightly greased baking dish.
Combine the vermouth, lemon juice, and melted butter and pour over the fish.
Melt the remaining butter in a skillet and sauté the mushrooms until tender, then add the onion and cook, stirring, another 2 minutes.
Spoon the onion mushroom mixture evenly over the fish and bake for 20 minutes or until the fish is opaque and flakes when lightly poked with a fork. Sprinkle with chopped parsley and serve.
Serves 4.

FISH IN SALSA VERDE

Low in fat, delicious to eat. A wonderful company dish.

6 tomatillos (6 ounces) husked and finely
  chopped or a 13 ounce can tomatillos,
  drained, rinsed, and finely chopped
2 to 3 Tablespoons finely chopped onion
4 ounce can chopped green chilies, drained or
  1 or 2 Jalapeno peppers, seeded and finely
  chopped
a bunch of fresh cilantro, chopped
1 Tablespoon lime zest

1/2 teaspoon sugar
1/4 teaspoon ground cumin
salt
freshly ground pepper
1 1/4 pounds fresh or frozen fish like tuna
  steak, etc. cut into serving size pieces
1 Tablespoon lime juice
1/4 cup hot or spicy olives, sliced
1/2 an avocado, seeded, peeled and chopped

Preheat oven to 450°F. Rinse fish and pat dry.
In a large bowl stir together the tomatillos, onion, chilies or Jalapeno, cilantro, lime zest,
and sugar. Combine cumin, salt and freshly ground pepper in a small bowl and set aside.
Place fish in a lasagna size baking dish and brush with lime juice.
Sprinkle with cumin mixture. Stir the olives and avocado into the salsa verde and toss on fish.
Bake uncovered for about 6 to 12 minutes, or until fish flakes easily with a fork.
Serves 4.

FILLETS OF ROCKFISH WITH CIPPOLINE ONIONS AND OLIVES IN PARCHMENT

From the fabulous Washington, DC cooking teacher Phyllis Frucht.

1 1/2 pounds rockfish fillets, cut into 8 pieces
1/2 pound rosted cippoline onions, coarsely
1 cup baby spinach leaves
1/3 cup kalamata olives, pitted, coarsely
  chopped
1/3 cup pine nuts, toasted

salt
freshly ground pepper
oregano, thyme, or tarragon for sprinkling
1 tablespoon extra virgin olive oil

Preheat oven to 375°F. Cut eight squares of parchment paper (fold a triangle to make a square) 12
to 14” each (or you can use aluminum foil). Cut in a heart shape.
Place fish towards the middle of one half of the paper. Sprinkle with cippoline onions and salt
lightly. Top with baby spinach leaves, kalamata olives, and pine nuts. Sprinkle with salt, pepper,
and oregano. Drizzle with a little olive oil. Fold the other half of the parchment over the fish and
vegetables and fold the edges to form a half moon shape and seal the packet. Place packets on
a cookie sheet and bake for 12 to 15 minutes or until done. Bring to the table and slash to open.
Serves 8.

(continued on next page)

Roasted Cippoline Onions:

1/2 pound cippoline onions, peeled and
   trimmed
1/2 teaspoon extra virgin olive oil
salt

freshly ground pepper
fresh herbs, optional

Preheat oven to 375° F. Trim the root end of the onion off. If hard to peel, drop in boiling water for a minute and plunge into cold water. Skin should slip off easily. Drizzle with olive oil and season lightly with salt, pepper, and fresh herbs. Wrap in foil and place in a small shallow pan. Add 1/4" water and bake for 35 to 40 minutes.

FRENCH SOLE

This belongs to the "best I've ever eaten" category.

4 large sole fillets - about 2 pounds
1 1/2 pounds mushrooms, wiped clean and
   sliced
juice of 1/2 lemon
1/3 cup chopped fresh parsley
1/4 cup melted butter or margarine

salt
freshly ground pepper
pinch of nutmeg
1 cup finely ground blanched almonds
1/2 to 1 cup dry white wine

Preheat oven to 500°F.
Lightly score the sole fillets by making parallel, diagonal lines with a knife on the skin side to prevent fish from contracting while cooking.
Place the sliced mushrooms, lemon juice, parsley, melted butter, salt, pepper, and nutmeg in a large bowl. Add the ground almonds, after forcing them through a sieve to remove the lumps. If mixture is too dry, add a little more melted butter or margarine.
Butter a large shallow baking dish and spread the mushroom mixture over the bottom.
Lay the fish on top of the mushroom mixture, arranging them close together but do not overlap them. Sprinkle with additional salt and pepper. Lift the fillets at the corners and pour in the wine. The dish is now ready to cook, but it may be prepared ahead to this point and refrigerated.
To store, cover the dish with buttered waxed paper, placing the buttered side directly on top of the fish. If chilled, the dish must come to room temperature before baking.
Bake the fish uncovered, on the middle rack of the oven for 10 to 12 minutes, or until fish flakes when lightly poked with a fork.
Serves 4 to 6.

POACHED SALMON OVER GAZPACHO

My friends Dana and Julie own Soirée, a very fine catering business in Owings Mills, Maryland. One of their recipes is more fabulous than the next. This is another of their unique recipes using the best fresh seasonal ingredients.

1 side of salmon or salmon filets - size will
   determine how many the recipe feeds
water
1 tablespoon salt

fresh parsley
fresh thyme
fresh dill

Rinse the salmon. Place in a pot large enough to hold it, then cover with cold water or white wine. Add salt and herbs. Don't use herbs if serving gazpacho, use TARRAGON. Bring water to a boil over high heat then immediately remove from heat. Let stand for 10 minutes. Remove fish from water, drain and refrigerate. Before serving, bring fish to room temperature. Serve on Gazpacho.

Gazpacho:

4 cups tomato juice
1 red onion - finely chopped (about 2 cups)
1 cucumber, halved, peeled, seeded -
   finely chopped (about 1 1/2 cups)
1 red bell pepper - finely chopped (about
   1 cup)
1 yellow bell pepper - finely chopped
   (about 1 cup)
2 tomatoes, seeded - finely chopped
   (about 1 cup)
1/4 cup champagne vinegar or white wine
   vinegar

1 1/2 tablespoons chopped seeded jalapeno
1 tablespoon chopped fresh basil
1 tablespoon chopped fresh cilantro
1 tablespoon chopped fresh parsley
1 clove garlic - minced
3/4 teaspoon hot pepper sauce
1/2 teaspoon salt
1/4 teaspoon black pepper

Mix all ingredients in large bowl. Cover and chill until cold, at least 2 hours. Can be made 2 days ahead. Keep refrigerated.

PECAN CRUSTED SALMON

4 salmon fillets
salt
freshly ground pepper
2 Tablespoons Dijon mustard
2 Tablespoons melted butter or margarine

1 Tablespoon honey
1/4 cup fresh bread crumbs
1/4 cup chopped pecans
3 Tablespoons chopped fresh parsley

Preheat oven to 450°F.
Sprinkle salmon with salt and pepper and place skin side down on a lightly greased 9" x 13" baking pan.
In a small bowl combine the mustard, butter and honey. Brush mixture on fillets.
In a small bowl combine the breadcrumbs, pecans and parsley.
Sprinkle over the top of the salmon.
Bake for 10 minutes or until fish flakes easily and is done.
Serves 4.

SALMON IN GINGER SAUCE

This recipe has quickly become a favorite for serving to company.

8 teaspoons grated fresh ginger
8 teaspoons oyster sauce
4 teaspoons fresh lime juice
4 teaspoons soy sauce (mushroom soy
  sauce is best)
4 teaspoons Oriental sesame oil
4 teaspoons dry sherry
1 bunch fresh cilantro, washed and dried

oil for brushing parchment
4 pieces salmon, about 1/4 pound each
1 bunch scallions, cut into 2" pieces and
  julienne
freshly ground pepper
1 lime, thinly sliced

Preheat oven to 425°F.
Prepare ginger sauce by combining all sauce ingredients and setting aside.
Take a piece of parchment paper or foil and lightly brush with the oil.
Place each piece of salmon on the parchment or foil.
Divide the sauce among the fish, season each with pepper, top with 2 lime slices, 1/4 of the scallions and several pieces of cilantro.
Bring 2 of the edges of the parchment or foil up over the fish and fold over and over until it touches the fish.
Fold the other edges, individually, over and over until fold touches the fish.
Place on a cooking or baking sheet and bake for 12 to 15 minutes (if using a thermometer, it should read 120 to 125°F). Do not overcook.
Serves 4.

SALMON IN HERB CRUST

3 large egg yokes
1/2 cup olive oil
2 Tablespoons fresh basil, chopped
2 Tablespoons fresh parsley, chopped
2 Tablespoons fresh tarragon, chopped
2 Tablespoons fresh dill, chopped
2 Tablespoons fresh cilantro, chopped
1/2 pound butter, softened
2 cups fresh made bread crumbs

salt and freshly ground pepper to taste
4 (6 ounce each) salmon fillets, boned and
    skinned or a 1 1/2 pound piece of salmon
1 cup fish stock
1 cup cream
1 bunch fresh basil, chopped
juice of 1/2 lemon
2 to 4 Tablespoons chopped cilantro

Place the egg yolks, olive oil, 2 TBL basil, parsley, tarragon, dill, butter, bread crumbs, salt and pepper in a blender. Mix the ingredients together well, adding more olive oil if it is too thick.
Place the mixture between 2 sheets of saran wrap and roll it out flat with a rolling pin.
Cut out 4 pieces the exact shape of the 4 fish fillets. Remove the saran wrap and place the crust on top of the fish fillets.
In a small pan place the stock and cream, and cook over medium heat 3 to 4 minutes or until reduced by half. Season with salt and pepper to taste.
In the blender place the sauce and bunch of basil leaves. Blend until like a juice. Add the lemon juice. Preheat oven to 400°F.
Place the salmon on a flat sheet, spray with Pam and bake (may take from 6 to 20 minutes) or until crust is crisp and fish just done.
Place fish on individual serving plates, sprinkle with chopped cilantro.
Pour the sauce around the fillets and garnish them with the basil leaves and red bell pepper.
Serves 4.

SOUTHWEST LASAGNA

2 to 3 pounds firm white meat fish, skin removed
1 cup chopped onion
2 Tablespoons canned chopped mild green chilies or 3 fresh Jalapenos chopped
salt
freshly ground pepper
2 fish or vegetable bouillon cubes – optional
24 tomatillos with outer husks removed
3 cups fish stock, from cooking the fish
1 bunch fresh cilantro, leaves only, chopped
freshly ground pepper
2 Tablespoons cornstarch

2 Tablespoons cold water
2 to 4 Jalapenos diced or half a 4 ounce can of chopped green chilies
2 cups low fat or regular sour cream
1/3 cup regular or low fat milk
1 Tablespoon canola oil
1 cup chopped onions
8 ounce can chopped green chilies
12 to 15 corn tortillas, torn into pieces
2 to 4 teaspoons hot sauce – optional
1 1/2 cups shredded or grated regular or low fat Monterey Jack cheese

Place fish in a large pot, cover with water, add chopped onions, chilies, salt, pepper, and bouillon cubes. Bring to a boil, reduce heat, cover and simmer for 15 to 20 minutes or until fish is done.
Remove fish, saving the stock and let fish cool. Cut fish into bite size pieces.
Place the tomatillos in the reserved stock with the chilies and simmer for 7 to 10 minutes or until soft. Cool, then puree tomatillos in a blender with the liquid from cooking.
Return the tomatillo sauce to the pan and stir in the seasonings and cilantro.
In a small bowl, combine the cornstarch and cold water.
Bring tomatillo sauce to a boil, reduce heat to simmer, and stir in the cornstarch mixture, mixing well. Continue simmering for another 5 minutes then remove from the heat and let cool.
Combine the sour cream and milk in a small bowl and set aside.
In a skillet heat the oil and sauté the onions and chilies and cook until onions are transparent.
Preheat the oven to 350°F and grease a 9"x13" baking pan.
In a large bowl combine the onion mixture, fish, and hot sauce if desired, mixing well.
Arrange 1/3 of the tortilla pieces in the bottom of the baking pan. Layer with 1/2 of the fish mixture, 1/3 of the tomatillo sauce, 1/3 of the sour cream, and 1/3 of the cheese. Repeat layers and top with remaining tortillas, sauce, sour cream and cheese.
This can be made a day ahead up to this point. To finish, bring to room temperature and bake.
Bake for 40 to 45 minutes or until bubbly and lightly browned. Let sit 10 minutes before serving.
Serves 8.

TUNA WITH MANGO SAUCE

3 pounds fresh tuna cut into 12 pieces
1/4 cup white sesame seeds
1/4 cup black sesame seeds
1/4 cup sesame oil
1 or 2 ripe mangos, peeled, seeded and cut into small pieces
1/2 cup red bell pepper, diced
1 small shallot, minced

1 1/2 teaspoons powdered ginger
juice of two limes
1 cup extra virgin olive oil
salt
freshly ground pepper
3 to 4 cups mixed greens for salads, washed and dried

Press each piece of tuna with white and black sesame seeds on all sides.
In a large skillet, heat the sesame oil over low heat and place the tuna into the hot oil.
Cook tuna for a minute on each side, turning until all sides are browned.
Keep cooking and turning until the tuna is done the way you like it.
Remove the fish from the pan and drain well on paper towels.
Cut each piece of tuna into thirds.
In a large bowl, combine mangoes, bell pepper, shallot, ginger, lime juice, olive oil, salt, and freshly ground pepper. Whisk until blended.
Spoon some of the sauce on each dinner plate and arrange tuna slices in a semi circle on each plate. Toss the salad greens with some of the sauce and arrange on the plate with the tuna and serve at once.
Serves 6.

BEEF, LAMB, VEAL

BEST BRISKET

Quick, easy, tastes wonderful, can be frozen - what more can you want in a main course.

3 to 4 pound brisket
16 ounce can jellied cranberry sauce
1 packet onion soup mix

1/4 to 1/2 cup water
freshly ground pepper

Preheat oven to 350°F.
Place the brisket in a large pan with a tight fitting lid. Mash cranberry sauce all over the top of the brisket. Sprinkle with powdered onion soup. Season with pepper.
Pour water underneath and around brisket.
Cover tightly and bake for about 4 hours, or until brisket is tender.
Cool and slice, and remove fat from gravy. Freeze with gravy or separately.
Wonderful when served over or with noodles.
Serves 6.

Hint: The fatter side of the meat is the "point" and the leaner side is the "flat".
When roasting, the point should be up. When reheating, the point should be down.

BOBOOTIE

This is a popular African dish that is great for company since it is best if prepared a day ahead.

20 dried apricots
1 cup golden raisins
3 1/2 pounds ground beef
4 Tablespoons olive oil
2 large onions, chopped
salt
fresh ground pepper
3 to 5 Tablespoons curry powder
1 teaspoon ground ginger
1 teaspoon cinnamon
1 teaspoon ground coriander

1 teaspoon cumin
3 Tablespoons apricot preserves
1 Tablespoon sugar – optional
20 sliced or slivered almonds
2 large tart apples, chopped – optional
zest of one lemon
1/2 teaspoon lemon juice
2 slices of white bread
1 1/4 cup pareve milk substitute
5 large eggs
6 bay leaves

Place dried apricots and raisins in a bowl of boiling water and let sit for about 20 minutes or until reconstituted, then drain well and slice apricots.
In a large skillet, sauté the meat and onions in the olive oil.
Preheat oven to 350°F.
Remove skillet from the heat and add apricots, raisins, salt, pepper, curry, ginger, cinnamon, coriander, cumin, apricot preserves, almonds, apples, lemon zest and lemon juice. Mix well.
In a small bowl, soak the bread in enough water to get it soggy, then mash the bread with a fork and stir into the meat mixture. Place mixture in a greased 11" x 13" baking pan.
Break bay leaves in half and stick them half way through the meat mixture, placing them every 2 or 3 inches. Cover and bake for about 45 minutes, checking after 30 minutes to see if meat is done. Remove bay leaves and discard.
Beat the eggs and milk substitute together until frothy and pour over the meat.
Continue baking, uncovered, until the egg custard has set – about 25 minutes more.
Test with a clean knife inserted into the custard. If the blade comes out clean, the dish is done.
Serves 12 to 20.

BUFFET SURPRISE

I have been serving this to company for over 35 years. People request it when I invite them to dinner. I can also make it days ahead and refrigerate it or make it way ahead and freeze it for 3 to 4 months. The flavor just gets better!

3 to 4 pounds boneless chuck roast
3 cans (28 ounce each) sauerkraut, drained
1 pound box dark brown sugar

28 ounce can tomatoes with liquid
1 peeled whole onion
1 cut up apple

Place the meat in a large (at least 5 1/2 to 6 quart) pot. Dump the drained sauerkraut on top of the meat. On top of that empty the box of sugar. Dump the can of tomatoes with liquid over the sugar. Place the onion and apple pieces around the meat.
Place the pot on the stove, cover and cook on LOW heat for about 4 to 5 hours, or until meat falls apart into small pieces and apple, onion, and tomatoes "dissolve".
Serves 8 to 10.

HINT: A level teaspoon of sugar added to a can of tomatoes cuts the acidic taste.

CURRIED LAMB

4 Tablespoons vegetable oil
4 Tablespoons margarine
3 to 4 pounds of lamb cut into 1" cubes
1 cup finely chopped onion
1 garlic clove, finely chopped
salt
1 apple, peeled, cored, and cut into wedges
1/4 cup curry powder (or to taste)
2 Tablespoons all purpose flour

1 cup peeled, chopped fresh or canned tomatoes
1/2 cup golden raisins
1/2 cup chicken broth
1 cup water
freshly ground pepper
1 cup pareve cream substitute
1 cup shredded coconut (optional)

In a large pot over medium heat, heat the oil and margarine and add the lamb.
Cook the lamb, turning several times, until no pink shows on the outside.
Add the onion, garlic, and apple wedges, stir and continue cooking until most of the liquid has evaporated.
Sprinkle the curry powder and flour over the meat mixture and stir until the meat is well coated.
Add the tomatoes, raisins, chicken broth, water, salt and pepper, and bring to a boil.
Lower the heat and simmer, covered, on low heat for 1 to 1 1/2 hours, or until meat is tender.
Skim off any fat, and stir in the cream substitute and the coconut. Cook just until the sauce is heated but do not let it boil, then taste and correct the seasonings.
Serve with cooked rice, chutney, chopped hard cooked eggs, and mashed bananas.
Serves 6 to 8.

ESPRESSO-CRUSTED EYE OF ROUND ROAST OR RIBEYE

This recipe was inspired by a recipe from the National Cattlemen's Beef Association and Cattlemen's Beef Board.

3 pound eye of round roast or 4 pound beef ribeye roast

Rub:
2 Tablespoons ground espresso (or favorite) coffee beans
2 Tablespoons packed dark brown sugar
1 1/2 teaspoons (sea) salt
1 teaspoon coarsely ground black pepper

Balsamic Sauce:
1 cup balsamic vinegar
 1/4 cup margarine, at room temperature
4 teaspoons all-purpose flour
1 cup canned beef broth (not concentrate)
1/4 teaspoon coarsely ground black pepper

 Preheat oven to 325°F. Combine rub ingredients and press evenly onto beef. Place beef on a rack in a shallow roasting pan fat side up. Insert oven-proof meat thermometer so tip is centered in thickest part of beet, not resting in fat. Add 1/3 cup or more beef broth to the bottom of the pan.* Do not cover the pan, or baste the roast. Roast for 1 3/4 to 2 hours for medium rare, 2 to 2 1/2   hours for medium. Remove meat when thermometer registers 135°F for medium rare, 150°F for medium. Place on carving board and loosely tent with aluminum foil. Let stand 15 to 20 minutes. Temperature will continue to rise about 10°F to read 145°F for medium rare and 160°F for medium. Skim fat from drippings and save drippings.
Bring vinegar to a boil in a small non-reactive saucepan. Reduce heat and cook over medium heat about 20 minutes or until reduced to 1/4 cup. Mix margarine and flour together in a small bowl until blended.
Add broth, reserved drippings and pepper to pan. Gradually whisk in margarine mixture until smooth. Bring to a boil. Reduce heat, simmer one minute, stirring constantly. Carve thin slices and serve with sauce.   *If using ribeye do not add beef broth while roasting and roast at 350°F.
Serves 6 to 8.

GRILLED LAMB CHOPS WITH CHILE GLAZE

8 lamb chops each 1 1/2 " thick or small
  lamb roast
1/4 cup red wine vinegar
1/4 cup orange juice
1/4 cup maple syrup or pancake syrup

1 to 2 Jalapenos, minced
1 Tablespoon cumin
3 Tablespoons chopped mint
1/4 cup fresh lime juice
 freshly ground pepper

Combine vinegar and orange juice in a small saucepan and bring to a boil over high heat.
Lower heat and simmer until reduced by half...about 20 minutes.
Add syrup, Jalapeno and cumin. Simmer another 5 to 10 minutes. Remove from heat. Add mint
and lime juice, then season with pepper.
Baste lamb chops with glaze and sprinkle with pepper or seasoned pepper.
Grill 6 to 7 minutes per side or broil about 5 minutes per side. Brush with additional glaze when
turning. Reheat remaining glaze and serve with chops.
Serves 4.

KONA-BLACKENED STEAKS WITH GREEN PEPPERCORN SAUCE

This recipe came from Phyllis Frucht, an old friend and well-known cooking teacher.

8 (8 ounce each) rib eye steaks 1" thick
3/4 Kona or Espresso coffee beans

1/2 cup Sichuan peppercorns or mixture of black
  and green peppercorns
1 Tablespoon kosher salt

Preheat the oven to 450°F.
Place the coffee beans and peppercorns in a spice mill or blender and process until coarsely
ground (about the size of a small grain of rice). Add the salt and stir well.
Dredge the beef on all sides in the coffee mixture.
Heat a cast iron pan to smoking and sear the steaks in the dry pan for 3 minutes.
Turn beef and place the pan in the oven for 5 minutes. Remove the pan from the oven and turn
beef again. Serve with Green Peppercorn Sauce and Garlic Smashed Potatoes.

GREEN PEPPERCORN SAUCE

2 shallots, finely diced
2 Tablespoons green peppercorns
1 cup red wine

2 cups chicken or beef stock
salt
freshly ground pepper

In a non-reactive saucepan, combine the shallots, peppercorns and wine.
Bring to a boil and cook until the wine is reduced by half. Add the stock and reduce again until
about 1 1/2 cups remain. Season with salt and pepper if desired.
Serves 8.

LAMB, HONEY & RAISINS IN PHYLLO

Start a wonderful new tradition by serving this fabulous dish for Rosh Hashanah.
A great recipe for entertaining from Shirley Rubinstein.

1 box phyllo
1/2 to 3/4 cup raisins (covered with hot water
 for 10 minutes, then drained)
1/4 cup olive oil
2 cups finely chopped onion
2 Tablespoons minced garlic
2 1/2 pounds ground lamb
2 teaspoons salt

freshly ground pepper
1 teaspoon cinnamon
1/4 teaspoon cayenne pepper
1/2 cup tomato paste
2 cups fresh chopped tomatoes
2/3 cup honey
1 cup margarine, melted

In a large skillet or sauté pan, heat the oil and sauté the onion and garlic over medium heat until tender – about 5 minutes, remove from heat, place in a bowl and set aside.

Add the lamb to the skillet and cook until no longer pink. Drain off any excess oil. Stir in the salt, pepper, cinnamon, cayenne, tomato paste, tomato, honey and the sautéed onions and the raisins. Mix well, and continue cooking another 5 to 7 minutes over medium high heat to blend the flavors and evaporate any liquid.

Drain well and cool to room temperature. Grease a 9" x 13" ovenproof pan.

Preheat oven to 350°F. Cut phyllo dough to fit a 9" x 13" oven proof pan and cover phyllo with a lightly dampened towel while working.

Brush a sheet of phyllo with melted margarine and place in the bottom of the pan.

Cover with another sheet of phyllo and brush this piece with melted margarine and then repeat until you have used 8 sheets of phyllo.

Spread filling over the phyllo and top with a sheet of phyllo and brush with melted margarine. Repeat until you have used another 6 or 7 sheets of phyllo.

Brush the top sheet with melted margarine and bake for about 40 minutes or until top is golden brown. Cool well, then wrap and freeze. To reheat, you may re-bake it while frozen, but it will take about 90 minutes. This recipe can also be made as individual phyllo triangles and served as a main course or appetizers. Bake triangles at 350°F for about 25 minutes or until golden and puffy. Serve warm.

Serves 8.

MARINATED LAMB

I like to make this for company since it is "started" days ahead and all I have to do is cook it.

2/3 cup olive oil
3 Tablespoons lemon juice
1 teaspoon salt
freshly ground pepper
3 Tablespoons chopped fresh parsley
1 teaspoon oregano

3 bay leaves, crumbled
1 cup thinly sliced onions
4 garlic cloves, thinly sliced
6 to 7 pound shoulder of lamb*, boned, slit
 lengthwise (butterflied), laid flat and
 trimmed

Three or four days before serving, make the marinade by combining the olive oil, lemon juice, salt, pepper, parsley, oregano, and bay leaves in a large shallow glass baking dish. Add the onions and garlic.
Lay the meat in the marinade, and spoon some of it over the meat.
Cover and let the meat marinate in the refrigerator for three or four days, turning the meat 3 or 4 times a day if possible.
Preheat the oven to broil, or heat your barbecue grill.
Without drying the meat off, place it fat side down, on a rack about 4" from the heat in the broiler or on your grill. Sprinkle the meat with salt and broil for about 15 minutes; do not baste.
Turn the meat over with tongs to avoid puncturing it, and moisten it with a little of the marinade. Sprinkle it with a little more salt. Broil or grill another 15 to 20 minutes.
The meat is done when it is pale pink inside with a dark brown crust.
Remember when you cut the meat to test it for doneness, it will oxidize and get darker (inside) after a minute or two. To serve, slice the meat against the grain into thin slices and place on a serving platter. Serve with cooked onions if desired.
Serves 8 to 10.
*If your butcher will remove the sciadic nerve, you can use a leg of lamb.

OSSO BUCCO

This Italian one pot dish is grand for cold weather dining, and can be made ahead or frozen.

1/3 cup all purpose flour
1 teaspoon salt
freshly ground pepper
3 to 4 pieces veal shanks with meat on bone
   ("osso bucco bones") cut in 2" to 3" piece
3 Tablespoons olive oil
1 large onion, chopped
1 1/2 cups chopped carrots
1 1/2 cups chopped celery

2 to 3 garlic cloves, crushed
2 tomatoes, peeled and chopped
1 1/2 cups dry white wine
1 teaspoon basil
1 teaspoon thyme
1 bay leaf
3 Tablespoons chopped fresh parsley

Combine the flour, salt and pepper, and dredge the meat in this mixture, shaking off any excess. Heat the oil in a large pot, and brown the meat on both sides. Remove meat and set aside, adding more oil if needed, heat it, and sauté the onion, carrots, celery, and garlic for 3 to 5 minutes.
Add the tomatoes, wine, basil, thyme, and the bay leaf, mixing well.
Bring the mixture to a boil, return the meat to the pot, lower the heat and simmer, covered, for about 2 hours. (If there does not appear to be enough liquid, add more wine.)
Taste and correct seasonings. Just before serving, remove the bay leaf and add the parsley.
Serves 4.

THREE SAUSAGES WITH CARAMELIZED ONIONS AND APPLES

12 sausages (2 to 3 oz each) -
   best if you use 3 different
   types of sausage
1/4 lb margarine
2 large yellow onions, julienned
3 Granny Smith apples, peeled,
   cored, and sliced

1/4 cup dark brown sugar
1/4 cup balsamic vinegar
1/2 cup brown ale or Guiness Stout
caraway seeds - optional

Boil or grill the sausages until cooked through. Set aside and keep warm.
In a large skillet, melt the margarine and add the onions. Cook over medium heat, stirring, until onions are transparent - about 3 to 5 minutes. Add the apples and cook
for 5 minutes. Add the brown sugar, vinegar, and ale, and cook over medium or low-high heat until the liquid is reduced to the consistency of syrup. Slice sausages on diagonal and serve over onions and apples.
Serves 6.

PICADILLO

This is a Spanish empanada filling (with a variety of tastes and textures) that can be used for tacos, stuffed green peppers, or just served over rice or noodles as a main course.

2 pounds ground beef
3 Tablespoons olive oil
1 cup chopped onions
1 to 2 garlic cloves, chopped fine
3 tomatoes, peeled, seeded, and coarsely
  chopped
2 cooking apples, peeled, cored, and
  coarsely chopped

4 ounce can chopped green chilies, drained
  or 1 or 2 fresh Jalapenos seeded and chopped
2/3 cup golden raisins
10 pimento stuffed green olives, cut in half
1/2 teaspoon ground cinnamon
1/8 teaspoon ground cloves
freshly ground pepper
salt
1/2 cup blanched slivered almonds

Heat 2 TBL olive oil in a heavy skillet over high heat.
Add the ground beef and cook, stirring constantly, breaking up any lumps in the meat.
When no sign of pink shows in the meat, add the onions and garlic, stirring well.
Reduce the heat to medium and cook for another 4 minutes.
Stir in the tomatoes, apples, chilies, raisins, olives, cinnamon, cloves, salt and pepper.
Simmer, uncovered over low heat for about 15 to 20 minutes, stirring occasionally.
In a small skillet heat the remaining tablespoon of olive oil over medium heat, tipping the skillet to make sure the bottom of the pan is evenly coated.
Add the almonds and cook them 2 minutes or until golden brown. Do not burn them.
Drain the almonds well and add to the meat mixture a few minutes before serving.
Serve over rice or noodles, or in taco shells.
Serves 6 to 8.

VEAL DUXELLES

1/2 cup olive oil (approximately)
1/4 cup margarine
1 large onion, finely chopped
2 shallots, minced
1 pound fresh mushrooms, wiped and finely
  chopped
1 Tablespoon lemon juice
3 cloves garlic, minced

1/2 cup chopped fresh parsley
2 to 3 Tablespoons tomato paste
salt
freshly ground pepper
1 large egg, lightly beaten
4 veal cutlets
3 Tablespoons margarine

Preheat oven to 350°F.

Using either parchment paper or foil, cut out 8 pieces 8" x 6" each, and brush one side of each sheet with olive oil (using about 2 TBL in all).

In a large skillet, melt the margarine and sauté the onion, shallots and mushrooms for 3 minutes. Add the lemon juice and cook another 5 minutes or until the mixture is dry. Then add the garlic and parsley, and cook another minute.

Stir in the tomato paste, salt and pepper to taste, and mix well.

Remove the skillet from the heat and quickly stir in the beaten egg.

Return the skillet to a low heat and cook, stirring, until the mixture is thickened. Remove from heat and let mixture cool.

Brush the veal with some of the olive oil.

In another skillet, heat the margarine and remaining olive oil and sauté the cutlets until nicely browned. Remove from the heat.

Place a large spoonful of the duxelles on each of 4 pieces of paper or foil and cover duxelles with a veal cutlet. Spoon the remaining duxelles evenly over the cutlets.

Top with the remaining 4 pieces of paper or foil, oiled side down and fold the paper or foil to enclose the meat. Then fold the edges over twice so the filling cannot seep out.

Place the "packages" on a baking sheet and bake for 15 to 20 minutes.

Serve each piece of veal still wrapped.

Serves 4.

VEAL MARENGO en CROUSTADE

This is the most breath-taking dish to present to a guest!

4 Tablespoons olive oil, divided
2 pounds veal cut into 1/2" cubes
salt
freshly ground pepper
2 1/2 Tablespoons all purpose flour
2 Tablespoons tomato paste
1 large garlic clove, crushed
1 cup dry white wine
10 1/2 ounce can chicken broth
1 celery stalk with leaves, chopped
1 teaspoon thyme
1 small bay leaf

1 pound mushroom caps, cleaned and cut in half
   if large
20 small pearl onions, fresh (peeled), canned or
   frozen drained
1 pint small cherry tomatoes, washed and
   stems removed
2 Tablespoons fresh parsley, minced - for
   garnish
Croustades: 2 (each 1 pound) loaves French or
   Italian bread or 6 small individual rounds
   of bread
1/2 pound margarine, melted

Heat 2 TBL oil in a large pot and sauté the veal cubes, in batches, being careful not to crowd them or they will stew. Turn, and brown on all sides. Remove from pot and place in a bowl.
After all the meat has cooked, return it to the pan along with the juices.
Stir in the salt, pepper, and flour, stirring to coat meat well.
Tie the celery, thyme and bay leaf into a piece of cheesecloth to make a bouquet garni.
Add the tomato paste, garlic, wine, broth and bouquet garni.
Stir, bring to a boil, reduce heat and simmer. Cover and cook for an hour.
Heat remaining 2 TBL of oil in a large skillet. Over medium heat, sauté the mushrooms until golden. Push them to one side and sauté onions, turning often, until a pale gold. Set aside.
To prepare croustades: Preheat oven to 350°F.
 Remove all crusts and slice each loaf crosswise into 3 equal cubes.
Cut a circle around the inside of each cube, leaving about 1/2" wall on all sides and bottom.
With a grapefruit knife, or knife, carefully remove center of cubes. Or hollow out center of individual loaves of bread.
Brush all surfaces with the melted margarine, and place on a baking sheet and bake 15 to 20 minutes or until golden and set aside.
When ready to serve, stir into the heated veal mixture the mushrooms, onions and cherry tomatoes, stirring gently just to heat through about 5 minutes. Discard bouquet garni.
Place croustades on serving plate and spoon some of the veal mixture into the center, allowing some of the veal to spill over onto the plate. Sprinkle with parsley.
Serves 6.

VEAL NORMANDY

3 sweet apples, peeled and chopped
juice of two lemons
4 veal scallops (about 1/4" thick)
salt
freshly ground pepper
1/2 cup all purpose flour

6 Tablespoons margarine
2 Tablespoons vegetable oil
1/3 cup Calvados or Applejack (apple juice can
  be used)
1 1/2 cup pareve cream substitute

Place the apples in a bowl, and pour the lemon juice over them and set them aside.
Season the veal with salt and pepper to taste, and dredge the scallops in the flour, shaking off any excess.
Heat margarine and oil in a large skillet, and brown the veal, a few pieces at a time, on both sides. Do not crowd the veal, and remove each piece as it browns. Keep the cooked veal warm.
To the same skillet, add the apples, lemon juice and Calvados or Applejack.
With a wire whisk, scrape up any pieces of flour that have stuck to the skillet and cook, stirring constantly over medium heat for 3 minutes.
Add the cream substitute and continue cooking until it is well blended into the sauce.
Reduce the heat and simmer the mixture until it is reduced by one half and coats a wooden spoon.
Correct the seasonings. Return the veal to the skillet, spooning the sauce over the meat.
Leave the veal in the skillet just long enough to heat it through. Serve hot with rice or noodles. Serves 4 to 6.

Notes

Meatless

BLACK BEAN CHILI

If you cook this until it gets really thick, it can also be used as a dip!

2 Tablespoons olive oil
1 medium onion, chopped
1 red pepper, stemmed, seeded, and diced
1 teaspoon dried oregano
1 teaspoon dried cumin
salt

freshly ground pepper
15 ounce can diced tomatoes
4 ounce can chopped green chilies (mild)
4 garlic cloves, minced
2 (14 ounce each) cans black beans
1/2 cup or more grated cheddar cheese - optional

Heat the oil in a large pot over medium heat and sauté the onion and red pepper.
Stir in the spices and tomatoes and cook for a few minutes over medium low heat.
Add the chopped green chili and garlic.
Continue cooking for another 10 to 15 minutes and stir in the black beans. Continue cooking and stirring for another 20 minutes. Sprinkle with cheese if desired and serve hot over rice.
Serves 6.

EGGPLANT MOZZARELLA

1 medium eggplant (about 2 pounds), washed
  and cut into 1/2" slices
1/2 cup all purpose flour
1/2 cup extra virgin olive oil (approximately)
16 ounce can tomato sauce

1 teaspoon garlic salt
1 teaspoon dried oregano
1 cup grated Parmesan cheese
1 pound Mozzarella cheese, sliced thin

Preheat the oven to 350°F. Dredge the eggplant slices lightly in the flour.
Heat the olive oil in a large skillet and quickly sauté the eggplant slices until golden brown on both sides, then remove the slices as they cook and drain them on paper towels.
Add more oil to the skillet as needed.
Place half the cooked eggplant slices on the bottom of a 2 quart casserole and top with half the tomato sauce and season with half the garlic salt and oregano.
Sprinkle half the Parmesan cheese on top of the tomato sauce, and top with half the Mozzarella slices. Make a second layer using the remaining ingredients in the order given above.
Bake the casserole, covered, for 30 minutes or until the sauce is bubbly and the cheese is melted.
Serves 4.

HINT: To eliminate the bitter taste from eggplant, soak the slices in salt water for 15 minutes; drain well, and then use in any given recipe.

FETTUCINE PHOENIX WITH ARTICHOKE HEARTS AND LEMON

1/2 pound medium wide noodles, cooked
  according to package directions until tender
1/2 cup butter or margarine
1 cup whipping cream
zest of 2 lemons

11 ounce jar or can of artichoke hearts packed
  in water, drained and chopped
salt
freshly ground pepper
1/3 cup fresh chopped parsley
1 to 1 1/4 cups fresh grated Parmesan cheese

While noodles are cooking, prepare the sauce by melting the butter or margarine in a saucepan with the cream, over low heat.
Remove the pan from the heat when the butter has melted and stir in the lemon zest, artichoke hearts, salt and pepper. Toss in parsley and Parmesan, mixing well.
Place the drained noodles in a large serving bowl, add the sauce, and toss until noodles are evenly coated with the sauce. Serve at once.
Serves 4 to 6.

LASAGNA WITH BLACK BEANS

2 (28 ounce each) cans plum tomatoes
2 garlic cloves, minced
1/2 cup chopped fresh cilantro
salt
freshly ground pepper
10 lasagna noodles - you can use oven ready
  (no cook) noodles if desired

3 (15 ounce each) cans black beans, rinsed
  and drained 3 times
3/4 vegetable broth
1 teaspoon ground cumin
1/2 to 1 teaspoon chili powder
30 ounces part skim ricotta
4 cups shredded Monterey Jack or
  mozzarella cheese, divided

Preheat oven to 375°F.
Drain canned tomatoes and place in food processor with garlic and cilantro. Puree.
Add salt and pepper to taste. Spray an 8" x 12" baking dish with non stick spray.
In a large bowl, combine beans with about 1/4 cup vegetable broth, cumin, and chili powder.
Coarsely mash beans until liquid is incorporated, adding broth if needed, and as needed.
In another bowl, combine ricotta and 2 1/2 cups of the shredded cheese.
Cook the noodles according to package directions. If using oven ready, just soak them in hot water for a minute or two to soften them.
Place enough noodles (about 5) to cover the bottom of the pan, slightly overlapping them.
Top with half the bean mixture, half the ricotta, and then half the tomato sauce. Repeat layers, ending with the tomato sauce. Sprinkle on the remaining 1 1/2 cups of shredded cheese.
NOTE: You may stop at this point, cover the lasagna, and refrigerate until the next day.
Bake lasagna, uncovered, for approximately 50 minutes or until lasagna is browned on top.
Remove from the oven and let sit for 5 minutes before serving.
Serves 6 to 8.

MANICOTTI IN CREPES

The crepes transform this into a light, delicate main course. Can be made ahead and frozen. The tomato sauce can be made, frozen and used on any pasta, fish, or chicken. For Passover use the Passover crepe recipe.

Crepes:

1 1/4 cups water
5 large eggs
1 1/4 cups all purpose flour
pinch of salt

1 teaspoon melted butter or margarine, cooled
additional melted butter, margarine, or
    vegetable spray, as needed to make crepes

Crepes for Passover:

1 / 2 cup less 1 TBL potato starch
1/ 2 cup less 1 TBL matzo cake meal
1/ 2 teaspoon salt

6 large eggs
1 1/ 2 cups water
1 Tablespoon melted margarine

To prepare crepes: Sift together dry ingredients. Beat eggs until light; and beat in 1/ 2 cup water and beat again. Slowly add 1 cup water to dry ingredients, whisking until smooth. Gradually whisk in melted, cooled, margarine and eggs. Whisk until smooth. Blend in blender or processor for about 30 seconds. Pour into a container and refrigerate for an hour, covered, or let sit, covered, at room temperature for an hour. Prepare as directed. Makes about 24 (8") crepes.

Sauce:

1/4 cup olive oil
1 cup finely chopped onion
1 to 2 cloves garlic, crushed
28 ounce can Italian plum tomatoes, with liquid
6 ounce can tomato paste

3 Tablespoons fresh parsley, finely chopped
2 1/4 teaspoons sugar
1 1/2 teaspoons oregano
1/2 teaspoon basil
1/2 teaspoon salt
freshly ground pepper

(continued on next page)

HINT: To avoid crying when peeling an onion: keep onions refrigerated; use a sharp knife; light a candle right next to area where you are chopping. When slicing a raw onion slice the area around the root last.

Filling:

2 pounds ricotta cheese - regular or low fat	2 Tablespoons chopped fresh parsley
1/2 pound diced mozzarella cheese	salt
1/2 cup grated Parmesan cheese	freshly ground pepper

Heat a 7" or 8" crepe pan over medium heat for a few minutes, then brush with a little melted butter or vegetable spray. Pour in just enough crepe batter to cover the bottom of the pan.
Cook the crepe until it is "dry" on top and barely light brown on the bottom.
Turn the crepe over and cook about 10 to 20 seconds.
Remove crepe to a large plate and repeat the process until all the batter is used.
Prepare sauce by heating the olive oil in a large skillet and sautéing the onions and garlic.
Add all the remaining sauce ingredients and bring to a boil. Lower heat and simmer, covered for an hour. This sauce can be used in any recipe calling for a Marinara sauce, and it freezes well.
In a large bowl combine the ricotta, mozzarella, and 1/3 cup Parmesan cheese (rest is for topping).
Add the parsley, salt and pepper, and mix well.
To assemble: pour some of the sauce into the bottom of a large shallow baking dish.
Place about 3 TBL of the cheese filling in the center of each crepe. Fold crepe in thirds and place it seam side down in the baking dish. Repeat until all crepes and filling is used.
Preheat oven to 350°F.
Cover the crepes with the remaining sauce, and sprinkle on the remaining Parmesan cheese.
The dish can be assembled in advance to this point and frozen or refrigerated until needed.
Bake the manicotti, uncovered, for 30 minutes.
Remove the pan to a wire rack and let cool for 5 minutes before serving.
If baking directly from the freezer, bake at 350°F for an hour or until thoroughly heated.
Serves 10 to 12.

Hint: Crepes can be frozen in a stack, but a sheet of waxed paper must be placed in between each crepe.

OMELET PIPERADE

2 to 3 Tablespoons vegetable oil
1 onion, thinly sliced
1 green pepper, thinly sliced
2 tomatoes, peeled and seeded, drained and
  diced
1 to 2 garlic cloves, minced

4 large eggs
salt
freshly ground pepper
1/4 cup minced fresh parsley
1 Tablespoon butter or margarine

Heat 2 TBL of the oil in a small skillet, add the onions and green pepper and cook over low heat until the onion is soft.

Cover the skillet and continue cooking the vegetables over low heat until they are tender, about 5 to 7 minutes.

In another skillet, heat a little bit of oil, then add the tomatoes.

Cook just long enough to let the juice evaporate (don't let them get mushy), then stir in the garlic.

Cook another minute, then place the tomato mixture and the onion mixture in a colander and let them stand for a few minutes.

At the last minute make the omelet by beating the eggs with salt, pepper and parsley.

Preheat the oven to 400°F. Melt the butter in a 10" omelet pan with an ovenproof handle.

As soon as the butter is foaming and almost turning color, add the egg mixture and cook over medium heat until the eggs are set on the bottom.

Spread the vegetable mixture evenly over the eggs and place the omelet pan in the 400°F oven for about 2 minutes, or until the top is puffed and brown.

Watch it carefully, as it takes only a short time to cook on brown on top.

Serves 2 to 3.

HINT: In making omelets, the butter should be hot enough to form a film that insulates the egg mixture from the bottom of the pan. If the butter is only warm, it will mix with the eggs, yielding an omelet that sticks to the pan and has the consistency of scrambled eggs.

PASTA PRIMAVERA

To "slim down" this favorite dish, substitute yogurt for heavy cream. A great accompaniment to grilled fish, or a light entrée on its own.

8 ounces fettuccine
1 Tablespoon olive oil
1 large carrot, peeled and thinly sliced
1/4 cup sliced scallions
1/2 pound fresh mushrooms, wiped
  and quartered
1 garlic clove, minced

2 cups fresh peas
2 Tablespoons finely chopped fresh parsley
1/4 cup water
1/3 cup whipping cream or plain yogurt
1 Tablespoon Dijon mustard

Cook pasta according to package directions.
Meanwhile, heat the oil in a large nonstick skillet over medium high heat and add the carrot, scallions, mushrooms and garlic.
Sauté, stirring, until the vegetables are crisp-tender, about 4 to 5 minutes.
Stir in the peas, parsley and water; cover the skillet and cook on low heat for 3 minutes more.
Remove skillet from the heat and stir in the yogurt and mustard, stirring until smooth.
Drain the pasta and place in a large bowl then toss with vegetable mixture.
Serves 3 as a main dish, 4 to 6 as a side dish.

RICOTTA PANCAKES

Since there is so little flour, the taste is quite different from regular pancakes. Great as an appetizer or for brunch.

15 to 16 ounce container ricotta cheese
  (low fat can be used)
4 large eggs
6 Tablespoons flour
2 Tablespoon melted and cooled butter
  or margarine

1 to 2 Tablespoons sugar
1 teaspoon vanilla extract
vegetable oil or non stick vegetable spray
  for cooking

Place all the batter ingredients in a blender or food processor. Process until smooth.
Preheat a large griddle or frying pan over medium heat and lightly grease or spray it.
Spoon about 2 TBL or more of batter, depending on the size pancakes you want, onto the griddle.
I like silver dollar size.
When a few bubbles have risen to the surface of the pancakes and the tops have "dried"
turn them over and cook for another few seconds. Pancakes should be very lightly browned.
Serve with jam, applesauce, or even yogurt, or fresh berries.
Makes about 30 small pancakes.

HINT: To keep sour cream, ricotta cheese, cottage cheese, or yogurt longer, store them upside down in the refrigerator so that air cannot enter the container.

SPANAKOPITA

This Greek spinach and cheese pie is so versatile - it can be used as an appetizer, vegetable, or even a main course.

2 (10 ounce each) packages frozen chopped
  spinach
1/4 cup olive oil
1/2 cup finely chopped onion
2 Tablespoons finely chopped shallots
1/4 cup finely chopped scallions
1/4 cup finely chopped parsley
2 Tablespoons dried dill weed

salt
freshly ground pepper
1/3 cup milk
3/4 pounds feta cheese, finely crumbled
4 large eggs, lightly beaten
2 cups (approximately) melted butter or
  margarine
16 sheets (1/2 pound) phyllo pastry

Preheat oven to 300°F.
Cook spinach according to package directions and drain well. Set aside.
Heat the oil in a large skillet, over medium heat and stir in onion, shallots, and scallions.
Cook, stirring, for 5 minutes. Stir in the spinach, cover the skillet tightly and cook 5 more minutes.
Add the parsley, dill weed, salt, and pepper stirring to mix well.
Cook, uncovered for 10 minutes or until all the liquid is evaporated and the spinach begins to stick to the skillet. Transfer the mixture to a deep bowl and add the milk. Cool mixture to room temperature. Stir in the cheese, and when mixture is cool, stir in the eggs and set aside.
Clarify the melted butter by melting it over low heat and discarding the milky residue on the top.
Brush the melted butter on the bottom and sides of a 9" x 13" x 2" baking pan.
Lay a sheet of phyllo on the bottom, being sure to press it into the corners and against the sides of the pan. (Some people prefer to cut the phyllo to just fit into the bottom and not go up the sides.)
Brush the entire surface of the phyllo with butter and lay another sheet of phyllo on top.
Butter it, and repeat process with 8 more sheets of phyllo.
With a rubber spatula, spread the spinach mixture evenly over the top layer of phyllo and smooth it into the corners.
Place a sheet of phyllo over the spinach and brush it with melted butter, and continue as before with the remaining phyllo and melted butter.
Trim off any excess phyllo from the sides and brush the top piece of phyllo with butter.
The dish may be frozen at this point if desired.
Bake, uncovered, for 1 hour. If baking directly from the freezer, increase the baking time to 1 1/2 hours. To serve, cut into 12 to 16 squares.
Serves 8 to 12.

SPINACH ROULADE

A dazzling meatless main dish for a luncheon or light supper.

Roulade:

3 Tablespoons butter or margarine
10 ounces frozen chopped spinach, defrosted
salt

freshly ground pepper
5 large eggs, separated
freshly grated nutmeg

Filling:

2 cups fresh mushrooms, wiped and sliced
1 Tablespoon minced shallots

2 Tablespoons butter or margarine
1 Tablespoon lemon juice

Mornay Sauce:

5 Tablespoons unsalted butter or margarine
3/4 cup sifted all-purpose flour
1 quart milk, scalded
freshly grated white pepper
freshly grated nutmeg

1 teaspoon salt
3/4 cup grated Swiss or Gruyere cheese
3/4 cup grated Parmesan cheese
1/4 cup whipping cream, as needed

Preheat the oven to 400°F.
Melt 3 TBL butter in a medium skillet and cook the spinach until all the liquid has evaporated.
Season with salt and pepper to taste, remove from heat and let spinach cool to room temperature.
Stir the egg yolks, one at a time, into the spinach, mixing well, and add nutmeg to taste.
In a mixer on high speed, beat the egg whites until soft stiff peaks form.
Fold the beaten whites into the spinach mixture and spread on a 10"x 15" jelly roll pan that has been covered with parchment paper that is lightly greased.
Bake spinach roulade for 10 minutes then remove the pan from the oven and turn roulade out onto a lightly dampened linen dish towel. Peel off the parchment and discard it.
While the roulade is baking, cook the mushrooms in 2 TBL butter in a medium skillet, until tender, then add the shallots and cook another 2 minutes.
Stir in the lemon juice and remove from the heat and set aside.
Prepare the Mornay sauce by melting 5 TBL of butter in a large pan over medium heat.
With a whisk, stir in the flour, then reduce heat and cook, whisking for about 5 minutes – do not let the flour burn.
Whisk in the scalded milk, beat and stir until sauce is smooth, then stir in seasonings, the Swiss cheese and 1/2 of the Parmesan cheese. If the sauce is too thick, whisk in a little cream and continue cooking until the cheeses are melted.

(continued on next page)

Combine the mushrooms with 1 cup of the sauce, and spread mixture evenly over the roulade. Start rolling the roulade up lengthwise, using the dishtowel to help you roll. Place on a large shallow baking sheet (or serving platter) and spoon about a cup of the sauce over the roulade, and sprinkle with the remaining Parmesan cheese.

If desired the roulade can be returned to the oven or placed under the broiler just long enough to melt the Parmesan and heat the roulade through. If the sauce and filling are still warm, this is not necessary. To serve, cut the roulade vertically into slices and pass the remaining sauce separately. Serves 8 to 10.

SHERRON'S ROASTED PUMPKIN AND SPINACH PENNE

Roasted cherry tomatoes may be added for additional taste and color. You may use acorn or butternut squash instead of pumpkin too. From Sherron Goldstein's *Fresh Fields: Entertaining With Southern Comfort*.

3 pounds pie pumpkin, peeled, cubed
2 tablespoons olive oil
16 ounces package penne
12 ounces bag fresh baby spinach, washed and torn
1 teaspoon grated fresh nutmeg
4 tablespoons unsalted butter
4 tablespoons olive oil

4 tablespoons fresh sage chopped coarsely leaves
1/4 cup fresh lemon zest
2 tablespoons lemon juice
1/2 cup toasted slivered almonds
salt
fresh ground pepper

Preheat oven to 375F. Toss the pumpkin in the olive oil and place in a foil lined baking pan. Salt and pepper to taste. Roast for 40 minutes or until browned on the edges. Set aside.

Cook the pasta in a larger pot of boiling water until al dente. Drain, DO NOT rinse, and toss with fresh spinach and nutmeg. Keep warm.

Place the butter and additional oil in a pan over medium low heat and stir until butter is melted. Add the sage and lemon zest and cook for a minute until crispy.

To serve, toss the pasta-spinach mixture with the pumpkin, lemon juice, toasted almonds, sage, and lemon zest, salt and pepper.

Serves 8.

Notes

Brunch

APPLE STRUDEL PANCAKE

A recipe from the Morning Star Inn, a bed and breakfast in a fabulous setting, with glorious antiques and exceptional food!

1 stick butter or margarine
5 to 6 large apples, peeled, cored, and sliced
6 large eggs, beaten
1 1/2 cups milk
1 teaspoon vanilla

1 cup all-purpose flour
3 Tablespoons sugar
1 teaspoon cinnamon
dark brown sugar to taste

Preheat oven to 350°F. In a 9"x 13" Pyrex dish, melt the butter in the oven for 10 minutes. Add the apples and bake another 10 minutes.
In a large bowl combine the eggs, milk, and vanilla, beating well.
Stir the flour, sugar and cinnamon into the milk mixture. Pour the batter over the apples and sprinkle with brown sugar. Continue baking for 30 minutes or until brown and puffed.
Serve at once.
Serves 8.

CREME CARAMEL FRENCH TOAST

From a B&B in Idaho Springs, Colorado.

2 Tablespoons corn syrup
1 cup dark brown sugar
1/2 cup butter
1 pound cinnamon raisin bread
6 large eggs
2 cups milk

2 cups light cream
1/3 cup sugar
1 Tablespoon vanilla
1/2 teaspoon salt
optional: sour cream, fresh berries

Begin this recipe the day before cooking.
Combine the corn syrup, brown sugar and butter in a saucepan, melt, stirring, until smooth and bubbly. Spread on the bottom of a 9" x 13" glass baking dish. Overlap the bread (like dominoes) on the syrup.
In a large bowl, combine the eggs, milk, light cream, sugar, vanilla, and salt.
Pour the mixture over the bread and refrigerate overnight - don't worry about any extra liquid in the dish – it bakes up like custard. Preheat oven to 350°F.
Cover pan with foil and bake for 45 minutes, remove foil and bake uncovered for another 15 minutes. The toasts should be puffed and golden.
Cut into 8 pieces and invert to serve. If desired, top with sour cream and fresh berries.
Serves 8 to 10.

EGG SOUFFLE

4 Tablespoons butter or margarine
1 green pepper, seeded, chopped
1 onion, chopped
1/2 to 1 pound fresh mushrooms, wiped and
  sliced thin
12 large eggs
1/2 cup flour

1 teaspoon baking powder
1/2 teaspoon salt
1 pint small curd creamed cottage cheese
1 pound shredded Cheddar cheese
1/2 cup melted margarine
3 tomatoes, sliced thin

Preheat oven to 350°F.
Melt the 4 TBL of butter in a large skillet and sauté the green pepper, onion, and mushrooms.
Drain well. Beat eggs well and add flour, salt, and baking powder.
Slowly blend in the cheeses and vegetables. Place in greased 9" x 13" Pyrex baking dish.
Top with sliced thin tomatoes. Bake for 45 minutes to 1 hour and 15 minutes or until set and
golden brown.
Serves 15.

GINGERBREAD PANCAKES

It is has been suggested that you can just use a buttermilk pancake mix and add the spices if
desired.

1 cup all purpose flour
1 Tablespoon sugar
1 teaspoon baking powder
1 teaspoon ground ginger
1/2 teaspoon salt
1/2 teaspoon baking soda

1/2 teaspoon cinnamon
dash of ground cloves
2 Tablespoons molasses
1 Tablespoon vegetable oil
1 cup buttermilk
1 large egg, lightly beaten

In a large bowl, combine the flour, sugar, baking powder, ground ginger, salt, baking soda,
cinnamon, and cloves.
In a small bowl, whisk together the molasses, oil, buttermilk and egg.
Slowly pour the liquid mixture into the flour mixture, whisking as your pour, until everything is
well blended.
Lightly grease a griddle or large skillet over medium low heat and spoon or pour the pancake
batter on when the griddle is hot. Cook the pancakes for about 3 minutes on each side, or until
done. This can be served with the Lemon Sauce from Shirley Ingersoll's Blueberry Pancakes.
Makes about 12 small/medium sized pancakes.

GRAVALOX

This impressive dish is a real winner and can also be used as an elegant appetizer.

4 pounds (center piece) fresh salmon, in 2 filets
2/3 cup salt
2/3 cup sugar
2 teaspoons coarsely crushed peppercorns
1 teaspoon coarsely crushed allspice
1 teaspoon ground cardamom
4 large bunches fresh dill
2/3 cup Dijon mustard

1/4 cup sugar
1/4 cup white wine vinegar
freshly ground pepper
salt to taste
1/4 cup sour cream
2/3 cup chopped fresh dill
2/3 cup olive oil

Pat the salmon dry.
Combine the salt, sugar, peppercorns, allspice, and cardamom in a bowl, mixing well.
Rub this mixture into the flesh side of the salmon.
Arrange a bunch of dill on the bottom of a large ceramic or glass dish.
Place one filet on the dill, skin side down. Place a bunch of dill over the filet and cover it with the second filet. Rub the remaining marinade over the skin and cover with more dill.
Scatter dill around the fish. Cover the fish with waxed paper and place a brick or cans or a heavy plate over it to weigh it down. Refrigerate fish for 48 hours, turning periodically.
To serve, remove filets and scrape off seasoning. Slice fish in very thin slices, diagonally, and serve with sauce.
To prepare sauce, combine Dijon, sugar, vinegar, pepper, salt, sour cream and dill. Gradually pour in oil, stirring and mixing well until it is smooth. Refrigerate sauce. It will keep for two weeks.
Serves 12 to 20.

OATMEAL PANCAKES

For a wonderful weekend breakfast treat that is also low in fat, try these surprisingly light pancakes, topped with fresh fruit or fruit flavored low fat yogurt.

1 1/4 cups skim milk
1 cup rolled oats
1 Tablespoon oil
4 large egg whites, beaten

1/2 cup whole wheat flour
2 Tablespoons brown sugar
1 teaspoon baking powder
1/4 teaspoon salt

In a medium bowl, combine milk with oats and let stand at least 5 minutes.
Add oil and egg whites to oat mixture, blending well.
Stir in remaining ingredients, mixing just until dry and they are moistened.
Heat a griddle over medium high heat and spray with a nonfat cooking spray.
Use about 1/4 cup of the batter for each pancake.
Turn when the top is covered with bubbles and looks somewhat dry.
Makes about 8 pancakes.

PUMPKIN PANCAKES WITH CIDER SAUCE

I first tasted these in Ohio, at a B&B (At Home In Urbana) owned by Shirley and Grant Ingersoll. Every morning Shirley made a huge supply of unusual pancakes - the lightest pancakes I have ever tasted.

2 cups all purpose flour
2 Tablespoons sugar
1 teaspoon baking soda
2 teaspoon baking powder
1 teaspoon cinnamon
1/2 teaspoon pumpkin spices
1/3 cup vegetable oil

1 cup canned pumpkin
2 large eggs
1/2 cup walnuts
1/2 cup raisins
1 cup sour cream
approximately 1 1/2 cups buttermilk to make a
    medium thick batter

Combine dry ingredients, then stir in oil, pumpkin, egg, nuts, raisins and sour cream. Mix well.
Stir in buttermilk - enough to make a medium thick batter, and pour onto a hot griddle or frying pan.
Makes a dozen large pancakes. Make syrup and serve hot.
Cider Sauce:
2 cups cider
1/2 stick margarine

2 Tablespoons cornstarch
2 Tablespoons mulling spices

Place all sauce ingredients in a pan over medium heat, and stir with a whisk constantly until blended. Place in a gravy boat and serve with pancakes. Makes about 2 cups of sauce.

SHERRON GOLDSTEIN'S CHEDDAR & SAGE BISCUITS

3 cups all purpose flour
1 1/2 teaspoons salt
2 Tablespoons baking powder
3 Tablespoons canola oil or Crisco
1 stick plus 1 Tablespoon butter,
    unsalted, cut into small pieces

1/ 3 cup fresh sage leaves, chopped
1 cup grated cheddar cheese
1 1/ 4 cups buttermilk
4 Tablespoons unsalted butter, melted

Preheat oven to 400°F. Place rack in middle position.
In a large bowl whisk together flour, salt, and baking powder.
Using your fingers or a pastry blender, work butter and shortening into dry ingredients until mixture resembles pea-sized chunks. Add cheddar cheese and sage and blend just until combined.
Gradually add buttermilk to bowl, stirring gently to combine. Gently knead dough to
bring mixture together into one cohesive ball. Turn dough onto a lightly floured surface and pat into a disc about 1-inch thick. With a 3""round cookie cutter cut biscuits and place on a baking sheet lined with parchment paper. Biscuits need to be touching each other. If remaining dough is rolled again for additional biscuits, they will not be as tender. Brush tops with melted butter and bake 18 to 20 minutes or until golden brown.   Serve hot. Makes about 18.

SHIRLEY'S BLUEBERRY PANCAKES WITH LEMON SAUCE

2 cups all purpose flour
2 Tablespoons sugar
1 teaspoon baking soda
2 teaspoons baking powder
1/3 cup vegetable oil

2 large eggs
1 cup sour cream
low fat buttermilk
1 cup or more fresh blueberries

Lemon Sauce:

2 cups water
1 cup sugar
1/2 stick margarine

2 Tablespoons cornstarch
zest from one lemon

Combine dry ingredients and stir in oil, eggs, and sour cream.
Mix well, and add enough buttermilk to make a medium thick consistency.
Add the blueberries to the batter while it is on the griddle.
To prepare Lemon Sauce: Combine ingredients in a saucepan over medium heat, stirring constantly with a whisk. When sauce is blended and thick, serve with pancakes.
Makes about 2 cups of sauce.

SMOKED SALMON CHEESECAKE

When I am feeling really lazy, I either omit the onions or don't bother sautéing them! This can also be used as an appetizer.

1 1/2 pounds cream cheese, softened to room
    temperature
4 large eggs
1/4 cup Half and Half or cream
1/2 cup minced onions, sautéed

1/4 cup fresh chopped dill, or 1/8 cup dried dill
    weed
4 ounces grated Swiss cheese
8 ounces smoked Nova salmon

Preheat oven to 300°F.
In a mixer, cream together the cream cheese, eggs, and Half and Half or cream.
Add the sautéed onions, dill, cheese and salmon and mix to blend all ingredients together.
Pour mixture into a greased 9" spring form pan.
Place filled spring form pan in a water bath - another pan (that it will fit into) with boiling water coming at least half way up the sides of the spring form pan.
Bake for 45 minutes, then turn off the oven and let the cheesecake cool in the oven.
Remove from oven when cool, cover and refrigerate or freeze.
This can be served warm, at room temperature, or cold, depending on whether you want to spread it on bagels, breads, crackers, etc. Or, cut it in slices and serve it like a piece of cake.
Serves 10 to 12. More as an appetizer.

SWISS BREAKFAST

Also known as Bichermuseli, this wholesome mixture is a distant cousin of the more familiar granola. For a treat add fresh blueberries or strawberries when they are in season. Since this mixture does not keep well, only make as much as you are going to eat.

1 1/2 cups old fashioned rolled oats
3/4 cup milk
1/4 cup raisins
1 apple, cored and grated but not peeled
1/4 cup orange juice

1/4 cup honey
1/4 cup plain yogurt
2 Tablespoons chopped nuts, optional
1 Tablespoon grated lemon peel
1 banana, thinly sliced

In a medium bowl, combine oats, milk and raisins.
Cover loosely and let stand at room temperature for an hour.
Fold in remaining ingredients, mixing well.
If desired, add 1/2 cup of fresh berries and serve with additional milk.
Serves 2 to 3.

WINE AND CHEESE OMELET FOR A CROWD

This "make ahead" dish makes two large pans, so one can be frozen for future use!

1 large loaf day old French or Italian bread, broken into small pieces
6 Tablespoons unsalted butter, melted
1 pound Swiss cheese, shredded
1 pound Monterey Jack cheese, shredded
16 large eggs
3 cups skim milk
1 cup dry white wine

4 large green onions, minced
1 Tablespoon Dijon mustard
freshly ground pepper
1/2 teaspoon red pepper
dash of hot sauce - optional
1 cup regular or low fat sour cream
2/3 to 1 cup grated Parmesan cheese

Spray or grease two shallow baking dishes.
Spread the bread over the bottoms of the pans and drizzle with butter.
Sprinkle with the Swiss and Jack cheeses.
Beat the eggs, milk, wine, green onion, mustard, pepper and red pepper and hot sauce (if desired) until foamy. Pour over the cheeses.
Cover dishes with foil and refrigerate overnight or up to 24 hours.
Preheat oven to 325°F.
Remove from the refrigerator about 30 minutes before baking and let come to room temperature.
Bake casseroles, covered, until set - about one hour.
Uncover casseroles and spread with sour cream and sprinkle with Parmesan cheese.
Bake uncovered until crusty and lightly browned - about 10 minutes.
Each pan serves at least 12.

Breads

BANANA BREAD

A delicious (and nutritious) way to use up over ripe bananas.

3/4 cup shortening
1 cup sugar
2 large eggs, lightly beaten
2 cups flour
1 teaspoon salt

1/2 teaspoon baking soda
1 1/2 teaspoons baking powder
2 large or 3 small very ripe bananas
3/4 cup chopped walnuts

Preheat the oven to 350°F. Grease and dust with flour a 9" x 5" x 3" loaf pan.
In a medium bowl, with an electric mixer at medium speed, cream together the shortening and sugar until light and fluffy. Beat in the eggs.
In another bowl, sift together the dry ingredients, and add to the creamed mixture.
Mash the bananas well, and add, along with the walnuts, to the batter.
Mix only until ingredients are combined; batter will be thick.
Spoon the batter into the prepared pan, and bake for an hour, or until well-browned on top, and loaf tests done. Turn loaf onto wire rack to cool completely.
Wrap the loaf in aluminum foil, and refrigerate for several hours for easier slicing, or freeze.

HINT: When using sliced bananas in any recipe, you can prevent them from turning brown by marinating them for a few minutes in the juice of any canned fruit or in a little lemon juice.

BEER BISCUITS

In many recipes beer can be substituted for water and in a cake recipe (if you use beer instead of water) the cake will be moister and stay moister, longer. Beer can be used in breads, batters, sauces, gravies, crepes, spreads, soups, and countless other recipes. When used in batters it creates a bubbly, light batter.
In marinades it acts as a tenderizing agent and flavoring ingredient. Beer makes for crispier pancakes and ultra light soufflés, and in other aspects of cooking beer brings out the natural richness and adds a subtle seasoning. Remember beer does not dominate the flavor of the dish, it merely enhances it.

2 cups biscuit mix   1/ 2 cup cold beer

Preheat oven to 425F.
Mix ingredients together in a large bowl and drop by spoonfuls onto a greased cookie sheet.
Bake until lightly golden brown.
Makes 10 to 12 biscuits.

CARAWAY SPOON BREAD

With an almost pudding like texture, this nutritious bread is almost a meal in itself - or the perfect partner to a hearty green salad or meatless soup.

3 cups milk
1 1/4 teaspoons salt
1 cup cornmeal
1/3 cup wheat germ
1 Tablespoon dried parsley flakes

1 teaspoon caraway seed
3 large eggs, lightly beaten
1 cup grated sharp cheddar cheese
1 1/2 teaspoons baking powder

Preheat oven to 350°F.
In a medium saucepan, slowly heat milk just to its boiling point. Add salt then gradually stir in cornmeal, stirring to avoid lumping. Cook over medium heat until thick, about 3 to 5 minutes. Remove from heat and stir in next 3 ingredients.
Slowly add eggs to cornmeal mixture, then stir in cheese and baking powder.
Pour into a greased 1 1/2 quart casserole and bake for 45 to 50 minutes. Serve hot with butter.
Serves 6 to 8.

HINT: For best results caraway seeds should be stored in the refrigerator.

CRANBERRY BREAD

2 large eggs, lightly beaten
1 1/3 cups sugar
1/3 cup canola oil
1 cup mashed sweet potatoes
1 teaspoon vanilla

1 1/2 cups all-purpose flour
1 teaspoon ground cinnamon
1/2 teaspoon ground allspice
1 teaspoon baking soda
1 to 1 1/4 cups fresh cranberries cut in half

Preheat oven to 350°F. Coat a 9"x 5" x 3" loaf pan with non-stick cooking spray and dust with flour.
In a bowl combine the eggs, sugar, oil, yams, and vanilla.
In a large bowl combine the flour, cinnamon, allspice, and baking soda. Make a well in the center and pour the yam mixture into it. Mix just until moistened. Stir in cranberries and spoon batter into the prepared pan. Bake for an hour, or until loaf tests done when a toothpick inserted in the center comes out clean. Cool thoroughly on a wire rack, wrap in foil or place in a freezer bag and refrigerate overnight for easier slicing (or freeze).
Serves 10 to 12.

ENGLISH MUFFIN LOAVES

Usually I avoid making breads with yeast since they require a little more time then I usually spend, but when I tasted this unusual bread (at breakfast) during a stay with a friend, I knew I would have to make it.

cornmeal
5 1/2 to 6 cups unbleached all purpose flour
2 packages active dry yeast
1 Tablespoon sugar

2 teaspoons salt
1/4 teaspoon baking soda
2 cups milk
1/2 cup water (bottled or tap, let sit overnight to dissipate chlorine)

Grease two 8 1/2" x 4 1/2" loaf pans and sprinkle the sides and bottom lightly with cornmeal.
Combine 3 cups of the flour, the yeast, sugar, salt, and baking soda and mix with an electric mixer for about 30 seconds.
Heat the milk and water in a saucepan to about 120 to 130°F, then pour the hot liquid over the flour/yeast mixture and beat for a few minutes. Slowly add the remaining flour, half a cup at a time, to make a stiff batter. Keep beating during this process.
Spoon the dough equally into the two prepared pans (dough will be very sticky). Smooth the tops and sprinkle the tops with a little cornmeal.
Cover the pans with a dishtowel and allow bread to rise in a warm, draft-free spot for 45 minutes.
Preheat oven to 400°F and bake the risen dough for 25 minutes.
Remove bread from pans immediately and allow to completely cool on a wire rack.
For easy serving, slice the cooled breads and wrap them in foil, then place in a plastic zip bag and seal. If freezing, remove slices needed for serving, and toast while frozen. This bread tastes best when toasted.
Makes 2 loaves.

CORNBREAD THYME MADELINES

1 1/4 cups flour
3/4 cup white cornmeal
1/2 cup sugar
4 1/2 teaspoons baking powder
1 teaspoon salt
1 1/4 cup buttermilks (or 1/2 cup
   buttermilk and 3/4 cup rich/larger
   or amber larger beer)

1/3 cup melted butter
3 tablespoons chopped fresh thyme
1 teaspoon freshly ground pepper
1 small can corn, well drained - optional

Preheat oven to 400F. Sift dry ingredients together.
Add milk (or milk and beer), melted butter to dry ingredients, mix slightly, add thyme, pepper, and mix well. Add corn if desired. Spray madeline sheets. Spoon mixture 1/2 way up each individual mold. Bake for 8 minutes, check often. They are done when slightly brown on edges and bottoms.

Makes 2 dozen.
HERB SOUR CREAM BREAD

Serve this tender, moist bread with soup and/or salad. It also makes delicious toast.

4 1/2 to 5 cups flour, divided
1/4 cup sugar
2 packages dry yeast
1 1/2 teaspoons salt
1 teaspoon dried marjoram
1 teaspoon oregano

1 teaspoon dried thyme leaves
1/2 cup water
1 cup sour cream, at room temperature
 6 Tablespoons butter or margarine
2 large eggs, at room temperature

In a large bowl combine 1 cup of flour with the sugar, yeast, salt, marjoram, oregano and thyme.
In a small saucepan, heat the water, sour cream and butter just until barely hot to the touch...do not overheat.
Pour melted mixture over the flour and with the mixer on medium, beat for 2 minutes.
Add eggs and 1/2 cup more of the flour and beat 1minute longer, then with mixer on low, beat in enough additional flour to form a soft dough.
Turn out onto lightly floured surface and knead for 8 minutes, working in more flour as needed.
Cover with a towel and let rest for 20 minutes. Preheat oven to 350°F.
Punch down dough, divide in half and shape into 2 loaves and place in 2 greased 8" x 4" loaf pans, cover and let rise in warm place until double...about 45 minutes.
Bake for 30 minutes or until browned on top, then remove from pans and cool on wire rack.
Makes 2 loaves.

JALAPENO CORNBREAD

To make a lower in fat version, use non-fat or light cheese.

1 cup yellow corn meal
1 cup all purpose flour
2 teaspoons sugar
1 teaspoon baking powder
1 teaspoon salt
1/4 teaspoon garlic powder

1 1/2 cups buttermilk
4 ounce can chopped green chilies, drained
1 cup minced onion
2 large egg whites
1 cup grated Monterey Jack cheese

Preheat oven to 350°F.
Combine all the dry ingredients in a medium bowl. Add the milk, chilies, and onions.
In another bowl combine eggs and cheese. Add the milk mixture, and the egg and cheese mixture to the dry ingredients. Stir just until blended.
Pour into a 9" square baking pan sprayed with a vegetable spray.
Bake for 40 to 50 minutes or until the bread is browned and firm.
For a twist you can add sun dried tomatoes or 1/2 cup chopped chives with the chilies.
This bread also freezes well.

Serves 8.
PUMPKIN BREAD

2 2/3 cups sugar
2/3 cup shortening
4 large eggs
2 cups pureed pumpkin
2/3 cup water
3 1/3 cups all purpose flour
2 teaspoons baking soda

1/2 teaspoon baking powder
1 1/2 teaspoons salt
1 Tablespoon cinnamon
1/2 teaspoon ground cloves
2/3 cup raisins - optional
2/3 cup chopped nuts - optional

Preheat oven to 350°F.
Cream sugar and shortening until light and fluffy.
Add next 3 ingredients, beating until smooth.
Combine flour with the next 5 ingredients and stir into pumpkin mixture until combined.
Add optional raisins and nuts. Spoon mixture into three 8" x 4 1/2" loaf pans.
Bake for an hour, or until loaves test done. Cool slightly on wire rack before removing from pans.
Wrap in foil and chill for easier slicing.
Makes 3 loaves.

ZUCHINI BREAD

I am not a big bread eater since I prefer sweets, but this bread tastes like cake. At times I serve it as cake. The zucchini is what makes this bread so delightfully moist.

2 small zucchini
3 large eggs
1 cup vegetable oil
2 cups sugar
2 teaspoons vanilla

3 cups flour
1 teaspoon salt
1 teaspoon baking soda
1 Tablespoon cinnamon
1/4 teaspoon baking powder

Preheat the oven to 350°F. Grease and dust with flour two 9"x 5"x 3" loaf pans.
Wash and dry the zucchini, but do not peel. Slice them and grate them in the food processor. Set aside.
In a large bowl, with an electric mixer at medium speed, beat the eggs until light and frothy.
Add the oil, sugar, grated zucchini, and vanilla, beating well.
Sift the remaining ingredients together onto a sheet of waxed paper and add to the bowl, mixing well.
Pour the batter into the prepared pans, and bake 1 hour. Cool the loaves in their pans on a wire rack for 30 minutes then turn the loaves out onto the wire rack to cool completely.
Wrap the loaves in aluminum foil and refrigerate for several hours for easier slicing and the loaves may also be frozen
Makes 2 loaves.

BRIOCHE

These are an excellent accompaniment to any egg dish, or just serve them alone with butter, jam, and coffee. They are a little rich to serve with a dinner. They can be filled and used as an appetizer or you
can make 1 large one instead of many small, fill it, and serve it for a main course. The freeze beautifully, indefinitely. To reheat, simply place brioches directly from freezer into a preheated 400°F oven for about 10 minutes.

1 package dry yeast	6 large eggs
1/2 cup warm water	3 cups sifted flour
1/4 cup sugar	1 1/2 cups additional sifted flour
2 teaspoons salt	1 egg yolk mixed with 1 TBL water
1 cup butter, at room temperature	

The day before baking: sprinkle the yeast over warm water in a large bowl; stir until yeast is dissolved. Add sugar, salt, butter, eggs, and 3 cups flour. Using a mixer beat at medium speed for 4 minutes, occasionally scraping sides of bowl and beaters with a rubber spatula. Add the additional 1 1/2 cups flour and beat at low speed for 2 more minutes, or until smooth…dough will be soft. Cover with lightly oiled foil and refrigerate overnight. The next day grease 24 3-inch muffin
tin cups or special brioche tins.
Remove dough from refrigerator - it will have a spongy consistency. Place on a lightly floured board
and divide dough in half. Return half to the bowl and refrigerate until ready to use. Working quickly, shape 3/4 of the dough into a 12" log. With a sharp knife, cut log into 12 even pieces. Roll each piece into a ball and place in the prepared tin. Repeat until all pieces are used. Using the same method, divide the other 1/4 of the dough into 12 smaller pieces and roll into smaller balls.
Dip your thumb in flour and press an indentation in the center of each of the large balls in the tins. Place a small ball in each of the indentations. Keep you thumb well floured to prevent sticking.
Cover tins with a towel and let rise in a warm place until dough has doubled in bulk – about an hour.
Then repeat procedure with remaining dough and let rise as directed. Preheat oven to 400°F.
Beat the egg with the water and brush on the tops of each brioche. Bake 15 to 20 minutes or until golden brown. Serve hot with jam and butter. Makes about 24 brioche.

HINT: When measuring flour or sugar, never use a liquid (Pyrex cup or one with a spout) measuring cup. You cannot get an accurate measure. Use the individual cups but do NOT dip them into the flour or sugar. Using another cup or spoon, place the loose flour into the right size measuring cup, heaping it in and level the top with a knife. Liquids should always be measured in a liquid measuring cup (one with a spout) and never in the individual measuring cups, as the measure will not be accurate.

salads

CANDIED WALNUT SALAD

1 pound walnut halves
1/4 cup honey
1/4 cup sugar
1/4 teaspoon salt
5 cups baby lettuce or torn mixed greens
a red bell pepper, seeded, stemmed and sliced
optional

2 tomatoes, sliced, or cherry tomatoes
1/2 cucumber, peeled and sliced
2 or 3 hearts of palm, sliced
1 small avocado, sliced
1/2 cup dried cranberries
1/2 cup (or more) chopped sliced mango
1 1/2 ounce soft goat cheese, crumbled

Preheat the oven to 350°F.
Line 2 baking sheets with aluminum foil and spray with nonstick cooking spray.
Place the walnuts in a small saucepan and cover with hot water, bring to a boil, and cook nuts for 5 minutes. Drain immediately in a colander and set aside.
In a 2 1/2 quart saucepan, bring the honey, sugar, 1/4 cup water, and salt to a boil.
Reduce heat to medium, add the walnuts, and stir until the mixture becomes dry - about 5 minutes.
Place the nuts on one of the baking sheets, spreading them out evenly, and bake at 350°F for about 15 minutes, turning them a couple of times - they should turn a light mahogany color.
Remove nuts from the oven and transfer them to the second baking sheet to cool.
When cool, separate them and set aside a cup for the salad. The remaining nuts can be frozen in an airtight bag.
In a large bowl, mix together remaining salad ingredients, including nuts.
Add just enough of your favorite dressing to lightly coat the greens. Toss and mix well, adjusting the seasoning.
Serves 6.

ELEGANT COLD RICE SALAD

2 (6 ounces each) packages chicken
  flavored rice
2 jars (4 ounces each) marinated artichoke
  hearts, drained
6 scallions, chopped

1/2 cup pitted black olives, sliced
1/2 cup mayonnaise
freshly ground pepper
1/2 cup diced pimentos

Prepare rice according to package directions and let cool to room temperature. Place artichoke hearts into a large bowl.
Stir in olives, scallions, mayonnaise, pepper, and pimentos and mix well. Add the cooled rice and mix well.
Refrigerate salad for 4 to 5 hours before serving.
Serves 12.

FROSTED FRUIT SALAD

As a rule, I do not usually serve gelatin type salads but this is the exception!

6 ounce box lemon gelatin
2 cups boiling water
2 cups lemon-lime soda
1 cup miniature marshmallows
20 ounce can crushed pineapple, drained with
  liquid reserved for topping
3 large bananas, sliced

2 Tablespoons flour
1/2 cup sugar
1 cup reserved pineapple juice
1 large egg, slightly beaten
1 cup whipping cream
1/4 cup grated cheddar cheese
3 Tablespoons grated Parmesan cheese

In a medium bowl combine the gelatin with the boiling water, stirring until dissolved.
Cool 10 minutes, stir in the soda and refrigerate until mixture starts to set, about 45 to 60 minutes.
Fold in the marshmallows, drained pineapple, and bananas and place in a 9"x 13" dish
Chill until firm.
Prepare the topping by cooking the flour, sugar, pineapple juice, and egg in a small pan over low heat. Cook and stir continuously until mixture is thick.
Remove the pan from heat and let it cool. Refrigerate topping until it is well chilled.
Beat the whipping cream until stiff and fold into the chilled topping mixture.
Spread the topping over the chilled gelatin mixture and sprinkle the Cheddar cheese and Parmesan cheeses over the topping. Place salad in the refrigerator and chill until serving.
Serves 10 to 12.

FRUIT SALAD FOR A CROWD

Originally I made this for "break the fast" but everyone loved it so much, I now make it for any buffet, brunch or dinner party.

l0 ounces frozen strawberries, defrosted
20 ounce can crushed pineapple with juice
11 ounce can Mandarin orange slices with juice
4 apples, diced

3 bananas, peeled and sliced
3 naval oranges, peeled, separated, and cut in
  half
1/2 of a 5 ounce box of vanilla instant pudding
    (dry mixture)

In a large bowl, combine all the ingredients.
Any local or favorite fruit can be added to the strawberries, pineapple, and pudding.
Cover and chill (after mixing well) overnight.
Serves 12 or more.

GREEK ORZO SALAD

1/2 cup pine nuts
1/2 cup currants
1/2 cup white wine, divided
1/2 cup olive oil, divided
1 onion, thinly julienne
1 pound fresh leaf spinach
2 Tablespoons chopped garlic
1/2 teaspoon nutmeg

salt
freshly ground pepper
1 pound fresh asparagus, blanched and sliced
1 Tablespoon Dijon mustard
1/4 cup lemon juice
1 pound Orzo pasta, cooked according to
    package directions
1/2 cup dried cranberries

Preheat oven to 350°F.
Toast pine nuts on a cookie sheet at 350°F for 8 to 10 minutes. Set aside.
In a small pan combine currants and 1/4 cup white wine and bring to a boil. Remove from heat and let sit for 10 minutes while currants absorb the wine.
In a skillet, heat 2 TBL olive oil and sauté the onion over medium heat until deep golden brown. Add spinach, garlic, nutmeg, salt and pepper and cook spinach just until it is wilted, turning carefully. Drain off liquid, mix with asparagus and set aside.
Prepare the dressing by whisking together the mustard, lemon juice and remaining white wine. Slowly, while whisking, drizzle in remaining olive oil, salt and pepper.
In a large bowl, toss orzo, currants, pine nuts, cranberries, and spinach mixture with the dressing.
Serves 12.

GRUYERE OR SWISS CHEESE SALAD

An unusual combination, that makes for a great appetizer or first course.

3/4 pound Gruyere or good imported Swiss
    cheese, finely grated
1 cup chopped scallions, including 2" of green
    tops, sliced
1/2 cup stuffed green olives, sliced

1/2 cup olive oil
2 Tablespoons wine vinegar
2 to 3 Tablespoons Dijon mustard
salt
freshly ground pepper

In a large bowl, combine the cheese, scallions and olives.
In a small bowl whisk together the oil, vinegar, mustard, salt and pepper.
Pour the well-blended dressing over the cheese mixture and toss until well mixed.
The salad should now stand for about 30 minutes at room temperature.
Cover the salad and refrigerate for at least 3 hours or overnight as the flavor improves with aging.
This is also a wonderful spread or great on open-faced sandwiches placed in the broiler with tomato, or avocado and broiled just until the cheese begins to melt.
Serves 6.

HERRING SALAD

My friend Shirley Rubinstein devised this unusual salad.

6 ounce jar herring in wine sauce, drained and
   sliced
1 Golden Delicious apple, peeled, cored, and
- finely chopped

1 cup finely sliced Bermuda onion
1/2 cup chopped pecans
1/2 pound fresh mushrooms, wiped and sliced
   optional

Dressing:

1 cup sour cream
1 cup mayonnaise
3 Tablespoons chopped red onion
2 Tablespoons fresh dill weed (or 1 TBL dried)

2 Tablespoons chopped fresh parsley
1 Tablespoon celery seed
1 head romaine lettuce or 1 pound fresh spinach,
washed and well drained

Several hours before serving combine the herring, apple, onion, pecans, and the optional
mushrooms in a large bowl.
In a small bowl, combine the salad dressing ingredients, mixing well.
Pour these over the salad mixture and chill for several hours.
A few minutes before serving arrange the lettuce or spinach on a large serving platter or on
individual plates and spoon the salad on top.
Serves 4 to 6.

JICAMA SLAW

An unusual low fat salad.

1 1/2 pounds whole jicama, peeled
1 medium carrot, peeled
1 whole red bell pepper, julienne or diced
1/2 cup red onion, sliced thin - optional

1 pint fat free yogurt
1 Tablespoon lime juice
1 teaspoon poppy seeds

Grate the jicama and the carrot into a large bowl.
Stir in the remaining ingredients and mix well.
Serves 4.

HINT: 1 pound Jicama equals about 3 cups chopped.

ORANGE AND RADISH SALAD

12 ounces radishes, trimmed
2 Tablespoons sugar
1 to 2 Tablespoons lemon juice
1 Tablespoon orange flower water or
   orange juice

salt
2 navel oranges
cinnamon

Shred radishes in a food processor or grate with a hand-grater. Allow excess liquid to drain off.
Toss the shredded radishes with the sugar, lemon juice, orange flower water (or orange juice), and
salt to taste. Chill. Peel and slice the oranges and arrange them decoratively on a serving plate.
Just before serving, sprinkle the radish mixture over the oranges and dust with cinnamon.
Serves 6 or more.

PAPAYA SLAW

4 cups regular or Chinese cabbage shredded
2 Tablespoons scallions, sliced diagonally
1 small ripe papaya, peeled and cubed,
   reserving the seeds
1 to 2 Tablespoons reserved papaya seeds,
   rinsed and drained

1 Tablespoon white wine or champagne vinegar
   (or white balsamic)
1 Tablespoon vegetable oil
1 teaspoon honey
1/2 teaspoon Dijon mustard
salt
freshly ground pepper

In a large bowl, combine the cabbage, scallions, and papaya, mixing well.
Coarsely grind or mash papaya seeds.
In a small bowl combine mashed seeds and remaining dressing ingredients, blending well.
Pour dressing over the salad, and toss to coat everything.
Serves 6.

SPINACH AND STRAWBERRY SALAD

10 ounces fresh spinach, washed, torn
   into pieces with stems removed
1 pint fresh strawberries, cleaned,
   hulled, and cut in half
1/2 cup sugar
2 Tablespoons sesame seed

1 Tablespoon poppy seeds
1/4 teaspoon Worcestershire sauce
1/4 teaspoon paprika
1/2 cup vegetable oil
1/4 cup cider vinegar

In a large bowl combine the spinach and strawberries. Place all the ingredients for the "dressing" in a blender or processor except the oil and vinegar. While blending (with machine running) slowly add the oil and vinegar. Blend until thick and smooth. Drizzle over salad, toss, and serve. Serves 6 to 8.

SPINACH SALAD

1 head leaf lettuce or romaine, torn into pieces
1 cup torn fresh spinach
11 ounce can mandarin orange sections, chilled
   and drained
1 cup white grapes, seeded and halved
1/2 cup toasted slivered almonds
1/2 cup canola oil

1/3 cup white wine vinegar
1 clove garlic, minced
2 Tablespoons minced frozen chives
1 Tablespoon curry powder
1 teaspoon soy sauce
2 Tablespoons packed brown sugar

In a large bowl, combine lettuce, spinach, orange sections, grapes, and almonds.
In a jar with a screw on lid, combine oil, vinegar, garlic, chives, curry powder, soy sauce, and brown sugar. Shake well before serving.
Just before serving, toss some of the dressing with the salad and serve the remaining dressing separately.
Serves 6 to 8.

SOIRÉE MIXED GREEN SALAD, SUGARED PECANS, & CHAMPAGNE VINAIGRETTE

If desired you can add fresh sliced strawberries, goat cheese, dried cranberries, and the sugared pecans.

1 or 2 bags mesclun or mixed greens, depending on how many you want to serve.

Sugar Pecans:

2 cups shelled pecans, walnuts or
  blanched almond
2 cups sugar
1/2 teaspoon kosher salt

1 tablespoon ground cinnamon
1/2 teaspoon ground nutmeg
1/2 teaspoon ground ginger
4 tablespoons butter or margarine

Mix all ingredients except butter, coating nuts. Using a 12" skillet on medium-high heat, melt butter in pan. Add nuts to melted butter. Stir continuously until sugar is melted and nuts are a golden brown color. Place a piece of parchment paper under a wire cooling rack. Remove nuts from skillet, and let cool on a wire rack. Store in an airtight container in a cool place for up to 2 weeks or freeze for 6 months. Makes about 2 cups.

Champagne Vinaigrette:

2 tablespoons champagne vinegar
1 tablespoon finely chopped shallots
1/4 teaspoon Dijon mustard
1/2 teaspoon salt

1/4 teaspoon black pepper
1/3 cup extra virgin olive oil
1 tablespoon finely chopped chives

Whisk together vinegar, shallots, mustard, salt, and pepper in small bowl. Add oil in a slow stream, whisking constantly until dressing is emulsified, then whisk in chives. Makes about 1/3 cup dressing.

TWO POTATO SALAD

3 red potatoes, scrubbed and cut into 1/4"
  chunks (do not peel)
4 russet potatoes, scrubbed and cut into 1/4"
  chunks (do not peel)
1/2 cup scallions, chopped
1 teaspoon fresh dill weed or 1/2 teaspoon
  dried

1/4 cup regular or low fat sour cream
3/4 cup regular or reduced fat mayonnaise
2 Tablespoons Dijon style mustard
2 Tablespoons capers, drained
salt
freshly ground pepper

Cook the potatoes in boiling water just until tender – about 15 minutes.
Drain well and toss in a large bowl with the scallions and dill.
In a separate bowl, whisk together the sour cream, mayonnaise, Dijon, and capers.
Pour over potatoes and blend thoroughly.
Season with salt and pepper to taste and serve at room temperature or chilled.
Serves 6.

Vegetables

ASPARAGUS WITH WILD MUSHROOMS AND ROASTED PEPPERS

This recipe was devised by chef/owner Alex Petrillo of the Piccolo Mondo Restaurant in Wilmington, Delaware.

1 pound fresh asparagus
2 Tablespoons olive oil
4 teaspoons chopped garlic
3 or 4 fresh shiitake mushroom caps, sliced
   or oyster mushrooms

4 Tablespoons julienne roasted red peppers
salt
freshly ground pepper

Wash the asparagus, remove tough portion of stalk and cut asparagus into 1" pieces.
In a large sauté pan, heat the oil over medium high heat for about 3 or 4 minutes.
Add the garlic and then the asparagus. Cook for 2 to 3 minutes and add the mushrooms.
Continue cooking for another 2 minutes, then lower the heat and add the roasted peppers.
Season to taste to with salt and pepper.
Serves 4.

BRANDIED CRANBERRIES

A very easy recipe that has been around for years, but is still a great accompaniment for so many main courses.

1 pound fresh cranberries
2 cups sugar

4 to 5 Tablespoons brandy
additional sugar - optional

Preheat oven to 350°F.
Wash the cranberries and drain them, removing any damaged berries or foreign objects.
Arrange the cranberries in a single layer on a large jellyroll pan.
Sprinkle the cranberries with the sugar.
Cover the pan tightly with aluminum foil and bake for an hour.
Remove the foil and scrape the berries and any liquid into a bowl.
Sprinkle the berries with brandy and additional sugar if desired.
When berries are cool, place in a glass jar or container and refrigerate covered until ready to serve.
This will keep for several weeks if refrigerated.
Makes about a quart.

CARROT CAKE RING

This "cake" is a delightful side dish, especially at a buffet dinner. After unmolding the ring, you can fill the middle with cooked and drained peas mixed with sliced fresh (or sautéed) mushrooms.

3/4 cup shortening
2 large eggs, divided
1/2 cup packed brown sugar
l teaspoon lemon juice
l Tablespoon cold water
l 1/2 cups grated carrots

l cup all purpose flour
1/2 teaspoon baking soda
l teaspoon baking powder
1/2 teaspoon salt
about 1/2 cup unseasoned bread crumbs

Preheat the oven to 375°F.
In a large bowl, with an electric mixer at medium speed, cream together the shortening, egg yolks, and brown sugar, beating until smooth and fluffy.
Add the lemon juice, water, and carrots, blending well.
Sift together the flour, baking soda, baking powder, and salt. Add to the carrot mixture, and mix well.
Wash and dry the beaters thoroughly, and in a small deep bowl, beat the egg whites until stiff. Fold into the batter until thoroughly incorporated.
Spray an 8 1/2" (4 cup) ring pan with vegetable spray and sprinkle with the bread crumbs to obtain a thin coating all around the pan; shake off any excess.
Pour in the batter and bake for 40 to 45 minutes, or until nicely browned on top.
Cool the cake on a wire rack for 15 minutes before turning it out of the pan.
This recipe may be frozen and is best if reheated while wrapped in foil.
Serves 8 to 10.

CARAMEL PECAN RICE

A friend sent me this and I use it a lot for company.

1/ 4 cup melted butter or margarine
1 cup pecan halves
1 cup dark brown sugar
3 cups cooked Basmati rice
4 large eggs, beaten
2/ 3 cup sugar

1 teaspoon salt
2 teaspoons vanilla
3 cups whipping cream, or paerve cream
1/ 2 teaspoon cinnamon
1/ 4 teaspoon nutmeg

Preheat oven to 350°F.   Place the butter in a 9 x 13 inch baking dish and melt in the oven.
Remove from oven and spread pecans evenly. Sprinkle with brown sugar. Combine all the remaining ingredients and pour on top of the sugared nuts. Bake for one hour.
Serves 8 to 12.

CARROT PUDDING

This doubles or triples or even quadruples beautifully. I usually do it times 4 (x 4) for dinner parties.

3/4 cup sugar (3 cups if x 4)
4 large eggs, separated (16 eggs if x 4)
3/4 cup grated carrots (3 cups if x 4)
1/2 cup finely ground almonds (2 cups if x 4)

1 Tablespoon grated rind of a lemon (whole lemon if x 4)
1 1/2 teaspoon sweet red wine (6 teaspoons if x 4)

Preheat oven to 325°F.
Beat together sugar and egg yolks until thick and lemon colored, about 5 minutes.
Add carrots, almonds, lemon rind, and wine. Mix well.
Beat egg whites until stiff, and carefully fold into pudding mixture.
Grease a 6 cup (or larger depending on how many "batches" you are making) casserole and coat with flour (or matzoh meal).
Pour pudding into casserole and bake for 65 minutes or until firm and well browned.
Serves 6 to 8.

HINT: Separate eggs while they are still cold, but allow the whites to warm up to room temperature before beating them.

CARROT RICE PILAF

1 Tablespoon olive oil
1/4 cup finely chopped shallots
2 Tablespoons pine nuts (I use more)
1 cup uncooked basmati rice
2 to 3 cups peeled and julienne carrots
3 teaspoons finely grated orange zest

1/4 teaspoon ground cardamom
1/8 teaspoon crushed red pepper (if using cayenne, use less)
2 1/4 cup chicken broth, heated
1/2 teaspoon honey
1/8 teaspoon salt

Heat the olive oil and sauté the shallots and pine nuts for 4 to 6 minutes.
Add rice, carrots, zest, cardamom, and pepper, and cook for 2 minutes, stirring frequently.
Add warm chicken broth, honey and salt. Cover, simmer 12 to15 minutes, or until liquid is absorbed.
Serves 4 to 6.

CHINESE OVEN RICE

What can I say about this dish - I have been making it for 36 years. When dinner guests call, they say "I know we're having Oven Rice, but what else are you preparing?"

2 cups long grain white rice - not instant
1/4 cup canola oil
3 Tablespoons soy sauce

1 package dry onion soup mix
8 ounce can sliced mushrooms - drain and save liquid

Preheat oven to 350°F.
In a 3 quart covered casserole, combine rice, soy sauce, oil, and onion soup mix.
Drain the liquid from the mushrooms into a Pyrex measuring cup and add enough water to make 4 cups of liquid. Add the mushrooms and liquid/water to the casserole, stirring well.
Cover and bake the rice for one hour. Stir well before serving.
Serves 8.

CHOCOLATE CHIP KUGEL

Since I am a "chocoholic" I serve this as a vegetable, although it could be a dessert.

1/2 pound medium twisted egg noodles
3 large eggs
3/4 cup sugar
1 pint sour cream, regular or low fat
1/2 pound small curd cottage cheese

1 teaspoon vanilla
2 Tablespoons butter, melted and cooled
1/4 cup crushed corn flake crumbs
1 cup semisweet chocolate chips

Preheat oven to 350°F.
Prepare noodles according to package directions then drain in cold water.
In a large bowl beat together the eggs and sugar, then add the sour cream, cottage cheese, vanilla and melted butter.
Grease a 9" x 13" baking pan and sprinkle with the crushed corn flake crumbs.
Fold the noodles and chips into the egg mixture and pour into the prepared pan.
Bake for one hour or until lightly browned on top.
Serves 8.

CONFETTI RICE

1 cup long grain white rice
10 ounce package frozen peas
5 Tablespoons butter or margarine
1 cup fresh mushrooms, wiped and sliced
1 small onion, finely chopped

1 teaspoon salt
freshly ground pepper
1/4 teaspoon rosemary leaves, crumbled
1/4 cup slivered almonds, blanched and toasted

Cook the rice according to package directions.
Cook the peas according to package directions, just until heated through but still firm.
Drain peas well and set aside.
Melt the butter or margarine in a large skillet over medium heat, sauté the mushrooms and onions until the onion is transparent, but not brown. Stir in the rice, peas and seasonings. Mix well.
Stir in the almonds, tossing to blend in with the other ingredients.
Serves 6.

CORN SOUFFLE

Another dish that I discovered at a party and had to have the recipe.

1 1/2 sticks margarine, melted
3/4 cup all purpose flour
3/8 cup sugar (scant)

7 or 8 large whole eggs
1 1/2 teaspoons baking powder
3 (14 3/4 ounce each) cans yellow creamed corn

Preheat oven to 375°F.
Blend together margarine, flour and sugar.
Add eggs, one at a time, beating well after each addition.
Add baking powder, beating well. Add corn and beat well.
Pour the soufflé into a greased 9" x13" Pyrex pan (3 quart).
Bake for 1 to 1 1/4 hours, or until brown.
If desired, you can prepare this dish early in the day, refrigerate, and bring to room temperature before baking. It also freezes well after baking.
Serves 15.

This is the smaller version of this recipe.

1 stick melted margarine
1/2 cup all purpose flour
1/4 cup sugar (scant)

5 whole large eggs
1 teaspoon baking powder
2 (14 3/4 ounce each) cans yellow creamed corn

Preheat oven to 375°F. Grease a 9" x 4" high two quart soufflé dish.
Blend margarine, flour, sugar, and add eggs, one at a time. Add baking powder and beat well.
Add corn and beat well. Pour into greased soufflé dish and bake at 375°F for 1 to 1 1/4 hours until very brown. Serves 8 to 10.

DHAL

This Indian lentil dish is very versatile and can be served as a main course with bread, vegetables and yogurt, or it can be used as a dip or served over rice. It freezes well.

1 cup yellow split peas, washed, rinsed in cold
   water and drained well
4 cups cold water
1 teaspoon salt
1/4 teaspoon turmeric
1/2 teaspoon red chili powder

1/2 onion, chopped fine
2 Tablespoons vegetable oil
1 teaspoon cumin
1/2 teaspoon fresh minced ginger
1 Tablespoon tomato paste
1 teaspoon ground coriander powder

Place the lentils, water, salt, turmeric, and 1/4 teaspoon chili powder in a large pot and cook, stirring, over medium heat.
Bring mixture just to the boil, stir to mix, reduce heat to simmer, cover, and cook for 15 minutes.
After 15 minutes, stir again, cover, and cook 30 to 45 minutes then turn off the heat and leave covered.
In a small skillet, heat the oil until hot and stir in the cumin, onion, and ginger. Lower the heat and stir in the tomato paste, 1/4 teaspoon chili, and coriander. Continue to cook and stir for another minute then add 1/2 cup of the pea mixture, mix well, and add this mixture back to the peas.
Correct seasoning if needed. Mixture will look soup, but will thicken when refrigerated. Serve hot or cold.
Serves 4 to 6.

EGGPLANT MELANGE

Eggplant lovers will love this tasty dish. Goes well with roast lamb or beef.

1 medium eggplant
6 Tablespoons olive oil
1 pound button mushrooms, wiped and
   trimmed
1 to 2 garlic cloves, minced

1/2 teaspoon or more fresh oregano, crushed
salt
freshly ground pepper
1 cup cooked green peas (fresh or frozen)
15 ounce can Italian tomatoes

Peel the eggplant and cut in half lengthwise. Cut the halves into vertical slices about 1/4" thick.
In a large skillet, heat 4 TBL of olive oil and sauté the eggplant slices until golden.
Remove eggplant and drain well on paper towels.
Heat the remaining olive oil and sauté the mushrooms and garlic.
Season with the oregano, salt and pepper to taste.
Sauté for 10 minutes or until mushrooms are tender but still firm.
Stir in the peas, the reserved eggplant and the tomatoes. Crush the tomatoes as you add them to the mixture. The dish may be made in advance up to this point. Simmer the vegetables for 15 minutes and serve hot.
Serves 6.

EILEEN'S FABULOUS NOODLE KUGEL

A superb dish guaranteed to have everyone asking for the recipe! The tiny noodles are the secret.

8 ounces fine (soup) noodles
5 large eggs
1 pound cottage cheese (regular or low fat)
2 cups sour cream (regular or low fat)
1 cup milk
cinnamon to taste

1 cup sugar
2 sticks butter or margarine, softened to room temperature
8 ounces cream cheese (regular or low fat) softened to room temperature

Preheat oven to 450°F.
Cook the noodles for 5 minutes in boiling water. Drain well and let cool.
In a bowl, beat the eggs.
In another bowl, combine the remaining ingredients and stir in the noodles and eggs.
Grease an 10" x 17" ovenproof baking dish and pour in the mixture.
Sprinkle a little cinnamon on top and bake for 5 minutes.
Reduce heat to 350°F and continue baking for another 45 to 50 minutes or so (depends on size of your pan) until lightly browned on top.
Freezes beautifully after cooling to room temperature.
Serves 8 to 12.

HINT: Adding salt to the water when cooking pasta is based on science. The salt raises the boiling point of the water, making it hotter, and cooks the pasta more consistently.

ELEGANT COLD RICE SALAD
A wonderful make-ahead vegetable or salad for any occasion.

2 packages (6 ounce each) chicken flavored rice and vermicelli
8 ounces marinated artichoke hearts
1/2 cup pitted black olives, sliced

6 scallions, chopped
1/2 cup mayonnaise
freshly ground pepper
1/2 cup diced pimientos

Prepare the rice according to package directions. Let rice cool to room temperature.
Drain the liquid from the artichoke hearts into a large bowl.
Coarsely chop the artichoke hearts and add them to the bowl.
Stir in the olives, scallions, mayonnaise, pepper, and pimientos. Add the cooled rice, mixing well.
Cover and refrigerate for 4 to 8 hours before serving.
Serves 12.

ELLIOTT ROESEN'S COUSCOUS

My cousin Roberta served this at one of her parties, and when I begged for the recipe she had me call Elliott (he's a famous Norfolk, Virginia caterer, and this is one of his popular dishes).

12 ounce box couscous	1/2 teaspoon vanilla
2 cups Farm Rich or Half and Half	1/4 teaspoon almond extract
1 Tablespoon honey	2 to 3 bananas, sliced
1 Tablespoon margarine	1/4 to 1/2 cup slivered almonds
3 ounces dried blueberries	1/4 teaspoon cardamom powder
3 ounces dried cranberries	1 to 2 Tablespoons dark brown sugar

In a large pot, bring to the boil the Farm Rich, honey, margarine, and couscous, stirring to mix well. Add the dried fruit, continue stirring, return to the boil, and remove the pot from the stove. Cover the pot and let it stand for 5 minutes.

Fluff the couscous, add the vanilla, almond extract, bananas, almonds, cardamom, and brown sugar, and mix well. Let it sit and serve at room temperature.
Serves 6.

ELLIOT'S SPICY CHICK PEAS

A nice side dish.

2 Tablespoons oil	pinch of cinnamon
1/2 teaspoon whole Mustard Seeds	freshly ground black pepper
1/2 teaspoon cumin seed	pinch of ground cloves
1 small onion, chopped fine	2 (15 ounce each) cans garbonzo beans, with
1 Tablespoon ground coriander	liquid
1/2 teaspoon ground turmeric	1/2 cup tomato sauce
1/2 teaspoon paprika	2 Tablespoons lemon juice
1/2 teaspoon salt	2 Tablespoons chopped cilantro

Heat the oil in a skillet, and sauté the mustard seeds until they pop. Stir in cumin and onion and sauté for a minute or two.

Add remaining ingredients, except for lemon juice and cilantro. Cook, stirring until well blended. Remove from heat stir in lemon juice and cilantro.
Serves 12.

GARLIC SMASHED POTATOES

What makes this really "smashing recipe" is the Wasabi - the green Japanese horseradish used with sushi!

6 baking potatoes or 9 medium red-skinned
   potatoes
3 Tablespoons olive oil
3 to 4 garlic cloves, finely minced
2/3 cup sour cream, regular or low fat

2/3 cup milk, heated
salt
freshly ground pepper
1 to 2 Tablespoons fresh made Wasabi (or
   white horseradish to taste) - optional

Scrub potatoes and cut into quarters or eighths; they do not have to be peeled.
Place potatoes in a large saucepan with cold water to cover and bring to a boil.
Reduce heat and simmer over low heat for 25 minutes or until fork tender. Drain well.
Heat oil in a small skillet over low heat and sauté garlic just until golden.
Watch the garlic carefully as it can burn quickly.
Combine potatoes with garlic and oil mixture in a large bowl and mash by hand or with a portable mixer. Texture should remain slightly lumpy.
Stir in sour cream, milk, and Wasabi or horseradish if using, and mash until well blended.
Season with salt and pepper to taste.
Serves 6.

GREEN BEANS GREEK STYLE

1 1/2 pounds fresh green beans
3 Tablespoons lemon juice
2 teaspoons Dijon mustard
salt
freshly ground pepper

3 Tablespoons olive oil
1 Tablespoon canola oil (or 4 Tablespoons
   olive oil in total)
2 Tablespoons finely chopped red onion

garnish: sliced red onions and Greek olives

Trim the ends off the green beans, keeping the beans whole. In a covered pot over medium heat, cook the beans in a small amount of water for just a few minutes. Remove from the heat while beans are still crisp. Drain beans and rinse in cold water several times.
Drain beans again, wrap them in a paper towel, and refrigerate until serving.
Prepare the dressing by whisking together the lemon juice, mustard, salt, pepper, and oils.
When well mixed, stir in the chopped red onion. Cover the dressing and refrigerate until serving.
To serve, place the beans in a serving dish, stir dressing again and pour over the beans.
Garnish with onion slices and olives.
Serves 6.

HANNA LEE'S SQUASH SOUFFLE THAT TASTES LIKE PUMPKIN PIE

When I first served this, it was the first time my family had ever had squash...I did not tell them what it was until after they had eaten the whole thing! This recipe can be halved, and it freezes beautifully.

2 (12 ounces each) boxes frozen cooked
   squash
2 sticks butter or margarine
1 cup sugar
1 cup all purpose flour
1 teaspoon vanilla

1 teaspoon cinnamon
1/2 teaspoon nutmeg
6 large eggs
1 quart Half and Half, cream, or pareve cream
   substitute

Preheat oven to 350°F. In a large saucepan melt the butter. Add the frozen squash and cook, stirring for 15 minutes. Remove from heat and whisk in sugar. Add flour, vanilla, cinnamon, and nutmeg, mixing well.
Add eggs if mixture is warm, not hot, stirring well after each addition. Stir in cream or substitute and mix well.
Pour into a greased and floured 9" x 13" baking dish.
Bake for an hour, or until firm in the center. Let sit a few minutes before serving.
If freezing, wrap well when squash soufflé is at room temperature.
Reheat at 350°F for about 20 to 30 minutes or until hot.
Serves 12 easily.

LEMON DIJON CAULIFLOWER

Bobbie Hinman is the well known author of "lean cuisine" cookbooks. This is her "updated" version of an old Polish recipe. It makes a pretty presentation and has a wonderful flavor.

1 medium size head cauliflower, washed well
1/2 cup plain nonfat yogurt
1 Tablespoon Dijon mustard
1/2 Tablespoon lemon juice
1/2 teaspoon grated fresh lemon zest

1 large garlic clove, crushed
2 teaspoons finely chopped fresh chives or 1
   Tablespoon dried chives
salt
freshly ground white pepper

Trim the leaves off the cauliflower and leave it whole. Place it on a steamer rack in the bottom of a saucepan large enough to hold it. Add enough water to come just up to the bottom of the rack, and bring to a boil. Add the cauliflower, cover, reduce heat and steam for 10 minutes or until cauliflower is just tender crisp.
In a bowl combine the yogurt, mustard, lemon juice, lemon zest, and garlic, mixing well.
Place the cooked cauliflower in a large serving bowl and spoon the yogurt sauce over the top of the hot cauliflower. Sprinkle with chives, salt to taste, and lots of freshly ground pepper. Serve immediately.
Serves 6.

NOODLE KUGEL WITH LEMON SAUCE

My friend Susan Shovers gave me this terrific recipe.

1/2 cup butter
8 ounces wide noodles, cooked and drained
8 ounces cream cheese, softened to room
  temperature
3/4 cup sugar
4 large eggs
1 cup milk
pinch of salt
1 teaspoon vanilla
1/2 cup golden raisins - optional

1 cup crushed corn flakes
1/4 cup sugar mixed with a teaspoon (or more)
  cinnamon
1/2 to 3/4 cup lemon juice
1 1/2 cups water
3 large eggs, separated
1 cup sugar
2 1/2 Tablespoons cornstarch dissolved in 1/4
  cup cold water

Preheat oven to 350°F.
Place the butter on the cooked noodles to melt.
In a blender or food processor, whip the cream cheese and sugar. Add eggs, one at a time, beating well after each addition. Add milk, salt, vanilla, and raisins if desired.
Stir cream cheese mixture into the noodles and spread in a greased 9" x 13" baking dish.
Top with crushed corn flakes and cinnamon sugar mixture.
Bake for an hour or until top is golden brown.
While kugel is baking, prepare sauce by combining lemon juice, water, egg yolks, sugar, and cornstarch dissolved in cold water.
Cook over low heat, stirring constantly until thick and smooth. Remove from heat and cool.
Beat egg whites until stiff and fold into completely cooled sauce.
Refrigerate until ready to serve with kugel.
Serves 10 to 12.

HINT: Lemons with the smoothest skin and the least pointed ends have more juice and flavor.

PARSNIP PUREE IN ARTICHOKE BOTTOMS

I had never eaten parsnips until a friend convinced me to try this recipe.

1 pound parsnips, peeled, sliced into 1/2" slices
1/2 cup butter or margarine, divided
1 teaspoon dried thyme
salt

freshly ground pepper
1 cup dry white wine
2/3 cup cream or pareve cream substitute
20 to 24 canned or fresh artichoke bottoms, well drained

Preheat oven to 350°F. In a 3 quart pot, place the parsnips, water to cover, and salt. Boil for 5 minutes, drain well, and pat dry. In a large skillet, heat 1/4 cup melted butter. Add parsnip slices, thyme, salt and pepper, and sauté for 2 minutes. Reduce heat to low and stir in wine. Cover and simmer until parsnips are very tender - about 10 minutes. Transfer parsnips and any liquid to food processor, and puree. Blend in remaining butter and cream, and season with salt and pepper to taste.
The recipe can be done up to one day in advance at this point, just cover and refrigerate.
Generously butter a large baking pan or cookie sheet that can accommodate all the artichoke hearts.
If some hearts don't sit straight, slice a little off the bottom to make them sit somewhat flat.
Fill a pastry bag fitted with a plain or star tip with the puree or using a spoon, pipe or fill each artichoke bottom. All of this can be prepared several hours ahead and then set aside at room temperature. Bake until heated through - about 15 to 20 minutes. Serves 10 to 12.

PINEAPPLE KUGEL

This wonderful recipe came from a caterer, who was one of my students.

1-1/2 cups sugar
4 cups farfel
6 eggs

20 ounce can crushed pineapple w/juice
2 sticks margarine, melted

Preheat oven to 325°F. Pour hot water over farfel in a bowl, and then squeeze it dry, and drain. Beat the eggs in a small bowl. Add all ingredients to the farfel and place in a greased 9 x 13" pan. Bake for about 45 to 60 minutes or until the top is slightly golden brown.
Serves 8.

POPPY SEED KUGEL

My Hungarian friend, Zsuzsi Zetlin, gave me this recipe of her mother's. Unusual and delicious!

4 large egg yolks
1 cup dark brown sugar
1 teaspoon cinnamon
1 cup golden raisins
1 Tablespoon olive oil
12 1/2 ounce can poppy seed filling
4 ounces unsweetened applesauce – optional
1 pound pineapple cottage cheese, small curd

4 ounces cream cheese or pineapple flavored
   cream cheese, at room temperature
18 ounces twisted wide egg noodles
12 ounce jar seedless raspberry (or other flavor)
   jam
3 cups of crumbled corn flakes
cinnamon
sugar
1/4 cup melted butter or margarine

Preheat oven to 335°F.
In a large bowl combine egg yolks, sugar, and cinnamon. Mix well. Stir in the raisins.
In another bowl combine the poppy seed mix, the applesauce if using, the cottage cheese and
cream cheese. Mix well. Lightly grease a 9" x 13" baking pan.
Boil the noodles according to package directions in water with olive oil. Drain well and run
noodles under cold water.
Mix the pasta with the egg yolk mixture and place a thin layer on the bottom of the baking
pan.
Spread with a thin layer of raspberry jam.
Mix the remaining noodles with the poppy seed mixture and pour over the jam.
Combine the crumbled cereal with cinnamon and sugar to taste and sprinkle over the top of the
kugel. Drizzle the top of the kugel with melted butter and bake for approximately 45 minutes or
until golden brown.
Serves 12.

RATATOUILLE

Serve it hot, cold, or at room temperature.

3 Tablespoons extra virgin olive oil
4 garlic cloves, crushed
1 Tablespoon finely chopped shallots
3 green peppers, washed, seeded and cut into
   1" strips
1 large Spanish onion, sliced
1 eggplant (about 1 1/2 pounds), cut into
   1" cubes

1 small zucchini, cut into 1" cubes
6 tomatoes peeled and coarsely chopped
6 ounce can tomato paste
salt
freshly ground pepper
pinch of cayenne pepper
2 teaspoons finely chopped parsley

Heat the olive oil in a large skillet and add the garlic, shallots, and green peppers.
Cook, stirring, over medium low heat for 5 minutes.
Add the sliced onion and cook 3 more minutes, stirring, then add the remaining ingredients and mix well. Cover and cook over low heat for an hour, or until the eggplant and zucchini are tender and the mixture is thick. Stir occasionally during the cooking time and correct the seasonings if needed. If not serving right away, refrigerate the mixture in a covered bowl. It will keep for several days and can be reheated if desired.
Serves 4 to 6.

ROASTED CHILI SWEET POTATOES

This is a great low fat, nutritious vegetable or snack.

2 or 3 sweet potatoes, washed
2 Tablespoons olive oil
salt
freshly ground pepper

1/4 cup regular or low fat mayonnaise
1 Tablespoon lime juice
1/2 teaspoon chili powder

Preheat oven to 350°F
Peel the potatoes and cut them in half lengthwise. Slice the potatoes into 1/4" slices and place in a large bowl. Drizzle olive oil over the potatoes, stirring to coat them all.
Place the potato slices in a single layer in a large jelly roll pan that has been sprayed with a non-stick spray. Sprinkle potatoes with salt and pepper to taste.
Bake for approximately 20 minutes or until potatoes are soft and golden.
In a large bowl combine mayonnaise, lime juice and chili powder.
Add cooked potatoes, and toss to coat (or prepare dressing in a small bowl and serve as a dip for potatoes). Spoon potatoes into a serving dish and sprinkle with additional chili powder to taste.
Serves 6 to 8.

SWEET POTATO CASSEROLE

6 to 8 sweet potatoes (to make 3 cups mashed sweet potatoes)
1 cup sugar
2 large eggs
1/3 cup milk

1 teaspoon vanilla
1/2 cup butter or margarine + 1/3 cup
1 cup packed brown sugar
1/3 cup all purpose flour
1 cup chopped pecans

Preheat oven to 350°F.
Boil the sweet potatoes with the skin on. Remove skin after cooking and mash.
Combine potatoes, sugar, eggs, milk, vanilla, and 1/2 cup butter. Beat well with an electric mixer until smooth. Spoon mixture into a greased, shallow, two-quart casserole.
Combine brown sugar, flour, 1/3 cup butter, and pecans. Sprinkle over top of casserole.
Bake for 30 minutes.
Serves 8 to 10.

SWEET POTATO SURPRISE

Remember holidays with sweet potato "balls" with marshmallow in the middle rolled in corn flakes? This is a new version of an old favorite.

2 (18 ounces each) cans sweet potatoes, drained
4 Tablespoons dark brown sugar firmly packed
1/2 teaspoon orange extract
2 teaspoons vanilla

1 teaspoon cinnamon
4 Tablespoons raspberry jam
1 cup crushed pecans
3 teaspoons melted butter or margarine -optional

Preheat oven to 350°F. Lightly spray a shallow baking dish with vegetable spray.
In a large bowl combine potatoes, brown sugar, orange and vanilla extracts and the cinnamon.
Mash with a potato masher until mixture is smooth and well mixed. Don't use the food processor.
Divide mixture into 24 portions and shape each into a half- inch thick patty.
Using a finger, make a 1/2" indentation in the middle of each patty. Spoon 1/2 teaspoon of jam into the indentation. Carefully shape the patty around the jam and mold into the shape of a ball.
Roll each ball in the crushed nuts.
Place in the prepared pan and drizzle lightly with melted butter or spray with non-stick spray.
Bake for 20 to 30 minutes.
Serve 10 to 12.

SHERRON"S EGGPLANT AND CHICKPEA TAGINE

Sherron Goldstein is the author of FRESH FIELDS and a fabulous cooking teacher.

1 large eggplant, cut into 1/ 2" dice	2 teaspoons ground turmeric
2 zucchini, thinly sliced	2 cups small red potatoes, quartered
1/3 cup extra virgin olive oil	2-1/ 2 to 3 cups vegetable or chicken broth
1 1/ 2 cups sliced onions	2 Tablespoons tomato paste
6 to 8 cloves garlic, chopped	2 Tablespoons bottled chili sauce
2 cups Crimini mushrooms cut in half	3 cups canned chickpeas, rinsed and drained
1 1/ 2 Tablespoons ground coriander	1/ 2 cup dried apricots
2 teaspoons cumin seeds	salt and freshly ground pepper
1 1/ 2 tablespoons ground cinnamon	1/ 4 cup fresh cilantro, chopped for garnish

Preheat oven to 425°F. Toss eggplant pieces and zucchini slices in a bowl with 4 tablespoons of olive oil. Add salt and pepper to taste. Arrange pieces on baking sheet(s) and bake for 20 minutes, turning occasionally. Do not let brown.

Heat the remaining oil in a large sauté pan. Cook the onion and garlic until the garlic turns a light golden color. Add the mushrooms and cook, stirring, for an additional 3 to 5 minutes until tender. Add the coriander, cumin seeds, cinnamon, and turmeric. Stir to mix well, allowing the spices to incorporate with the onions and garlic.

Add the potatoes and cook for 3 minutes, stirring, occasionally. Pour in the vegetable broth and tomato paste, cover and cook for 20 minutes (or more) on a medium simmer. The sauce should begin to thicken.

Add the eggplant, zucchini, chili sauce, apricots, and chickpeas, mixing well. Add salt and pepper if needed, to taste. Partially cover and cook another 10 to 15 minutes. If tagine becomes too dry add more broth. Sprinkle with cilantro and serve. Serves 8 to 10.

Desserts

APPLE WALNUT TORTE WITH CARAMEL RUM SAUCE

This wonderful combination will dazzle family and friends...but it's so easy to make.

1 cup all purpose flour
1 teaspoon baking soda
1 teaspoon ground cinnamon
1/2 teaspoon salt
1 cup sugar
1/4 cup unsalted butter or margarine, softened to room temperature
1 large egg, lightly beaten

1 1/2 cups chopped, peeled apples (2 or 3 large apples)
1/2 cup chopped walnuts
1/2 cup whipping cream or pareve substitute
1 stick unsalted butter or margarine
1/2 cup dark brown sugar, packed
1/2 cup sugar
3 Tablespoons dark rum

Preheat oven to 350°F. Grease an 8" x 2" round cake pan.
Sift the first 4 ingredients into a medium bowl.
Using an electric mixer, beat together the sugar and butter until blended. Add the egg and beat well. Stir in the dry ingredients, then apples and nuts.
Pour batter into prepared pan and bake for 45 minutes or until tester inserted into center comes out clean. Cool slightly on a wire rack. Cake can be made a day ahead. Wrap when completely cool.
To prepare sauce: combine cream, butter, and both sugars in a heavy, medium saucepan over medium heat. Stir until butter melts and sugars dissolve.
Increase heat and boil until slightly thickened, whisking occasionally, for about 3 minutes. Stir in rum. Cool sauce slightly.
Slice torte and serve warm or at room temperature with sauce and ice cream or yogurt.
Serves 6.

HINT: To keep brown sugar from hardening, store it in a container with a tight fitting lid with a piece of bread.

CHOCOLATE GUINNESS CAKE

This rich, moist cake came from Chef James Clark. It makes 3 cakes, so eat one and freeze two!

2 cups stout (such as Guinness)
4 sticks unsalted butter
1 1/2 cups unsweetened cocoa powder
4 cups all purpose flour
4 cups sugar

1 tablespoon baking soda
4 large eggs
1 1/3 cups sour cream

Preheat oven to 350°F. Butter three 8-inch round cake pans with 2-inch-high sides.
Line pans with parchment paper, and butter paper.
Bring 2 cups stout and 2 cups butter to simmer in heavy large saucepan over medium heat.
Add cocoa powder and whisk until mixture is smooth. Cool slightly.
Whisk flour, sugar, baking soda, and 1 1/2 teaspoons salt in large bowl to blend.
Using electric mixer, beat eggs and sour cream in another large bowl to blend.
Add stout-chocolate mixture to egg mixture and beat just to combine.
Add flour mixture and beat briefly on slow speed. Using rubber spatula, fold batter until completely combined. Divide batter equally among prepared pans. Bake cakes until tester inserted into center of cakes comes out clean, about 35 minutes. Transfer cakes to rack; cool 10 minutes.
Turn cakes out onto rack and cool completely.

ALMOND CAKE

1/2 cup butter, softened
1/2 cup sugar
10 1/2 ounces pure almond paste
3 large eggs

2 1/2 tablespoons flour
1/4 teaspoon salt
2 1/2 tablespoons kirsch
confectioners' sugar for dusting

Preheat oven to 300°F. Be sure the oven rack is in the middle of the oven.
Grease an 8" by 2" round cake pan. Line bottom of cake pan with a round of parchment paper or wax paper and grease paper.
Using an electric mixer beat together butter and sugar until light and fluffy. Add the almond paste, 1 tablespoon at a time, beating well after each addition until incorporated.
Add eggs one at a time, beating well after each addition. Beat in flour, salt, and kirsch just until blended. Pour batter into prepared pan and bake 50 minutes or until a toothpick inserted in the center comes out clean.
Carefully remove cake from the pan onto a wire rack, discarding the paper, and cool. Dust cake generously with sugar. Serves 8.

BOURBON STREET FUDGE CAKE

Adapted from a fabulous dessert I had at High Meadows Inn in Scottsville, Virginia.
Can be served with a cream cheese frosting, fresh raspberries or strawberries.

1 3/4 cup brewed coffee (water can be substituted)
1/4 cup bourbon
5 ounces unsweetened chocolate
2 sticks butter or margarine, cut into small pieces

2 cups sugar
2 cups all purpose flour
1 1/2 teaspoons baking soda
salt
2 large eggs, lightly beaten
1 teaspoon vanilla

Preheat oven to 275°F.
Grease and flour two 9"x 2" round cake pans.
In the top of a double boiler over simmering water, melt together the coffee, bourbon, and chocolate. Whisk in the butter, then remove from heat and beat in the sugar.
Sift together the flour, baking soda, and salt. Add to the coffee mixture, mixing well.
Stir in the eggs and vanilla and after mixing, pour into the cake pans.
Bake for 1 1/2 hours or until a cake tester comes out clean.
Cool on wire racks, sprinkle tops with confectioner's sugar, and serve with whipped cream if desired.
Makes 2 cakes, each serving 12.

Hint: Using light colored metal pans for baking unless otherwise specified. If you use dark metal pans, including nonstick, the baked goods will likely brown more and the cooking times may be shorter.

CHOCOLATE GATEAU

The very first French dessert I ever learned to make. It's very rich, and freezes well.

2 Tablespoons dark rum
2/3 cup semi sweet chocolate morsels
1 stick unsalted butter or margarine, softened
2/3 cup sugar
3 large eggs, separated
pinch of salt
1/3 cup pulverized blanched almonds
1/4 teaspoon almond extract

1/4 teaspoon cream of tartar
2 Tablespoons sugar
3/4 cup cake flour
1/2 pound margarine or butter, softened
1 pound sifted confectioner's sugar
3 large egg yolks
3 ounces dark sweet chocolate melted and cooled
1 Tablespoon dark rum

Preheat oven to 350°F. All ingredients should be measured and ready before you begin.
Melt the chocolate and rum in a double boiler over low heat. Set aside.
Grease and flour an 8" round spring form pan.
Cream together the butter and sugar until soft and fluffy - about 5 minutes. Beat in the yolks.
In another bowl, beat the egg whites and cream of tartar until they hold a peak.
Add 2 TBL of sugar and beat for another minute until whites are smooth and shiny, and hold a peak. Set aside.
Stir chocolate and add to the butter, sugar, egg yolk mixture.
Fold in the almonds, almond extract, flour and salt.
With a rubber spatula, stir in 1/4 of the beaten egg whites to soften the batter.
Place the remaining whites on top of the batter and carefully fold in.
Place batter in the prepared pan and bake for 25 minutes. If not done, bake a few minutes more.
Remove cake from the oven and cool in the pan for 10 minutes. Remove from the pan and cool on a rack for about two hours before icing.
To prepare icing, cream butter or margarine until soft, gradually adding the confectioner's sugar and beat well to blend. Add the yolks slowly, one at a time. (If you feel funny using raw eggs, buy either pasturized egg yolks, or place egg yolks in a microwave safe bowl with 1 TBL water, 1 TBL white wine, and a tsp of lemon juice. Zap on low for about 8 to 10 seconds, then beat again and use in recipe as directed.)
Stir in cooled melted chocolate a little at a time, then add the rum. Beat well then ice the cake.
Serves 10.

HINT: Add a pinch of baking powder to confectioner's sugar icings. This keeps the icing from getting hard and dry.

CHOCOLATE MOUSSE CAKE

Not as hard as it looks and well worth the effort! The chocolate cake is a good basic cake to make without the filling!

Cake:

1/2 cup sifted unsweetened cocoa
3/4 cup boiling water
1 3/4 cup sifted cake flour
1 3/4 cup sugar
1 1/2 teaspoon baking soda
pinch of salt

1/2 cup vegetable oil
7 large egg yolks
2 teaspoons vanilla
8 large egg whites at room temperature
1/2 teaspoon cream of tartar

Chocolate Mousse:

3 cups heavy cream or pareve cream substitute
1 1/2 cups sifted confectioner's sugar
3/4 cup unsweetened cocoa
1 1/2 teaspoons vanilla

1/2 teaspoon rum
1 teaspoon unflavored gelatin
2 Tablespoons cold water

Preheat oven to 325°F.
Place cocoa in a small bowl and add the boiling water, stirring until smooth. Let cocoa cool for 20 minutes. In a large bowl, sift together the flour, sugar, baking soda and salt.
Make a well in the center and pour in the oil, yolks, vanilla and cooled cocoa mixture.
Beat with mixer or spoon just until smooth.
Place egg whites in a large bowl. Sprinkle cream of tartar over egg whites and beat at high speed until stiff peaks form. Gently fold a third of the cake batter into the egg whites with a rubber spatula. Then fold in remaining whites.
Turn mixture into an ungreased 10" tube pan and bake 60 minutes. Cool completely.
For the mousse, pour cream into a large bowl and refrigerate until very cold - about 30 minutes.
Add sugar, cocoa, vanilla, and rum to cream and beat until stiff with a mixer. Refrigerate.
Sprinkle gelatin over 2 Tablespoons cold water (to soften) in a small pot and then heat over hot water, stirring until it dissolves. Let it cool.
To fill cake, cut a slice horizontally 1" down from the top. Set aside.
With a sharp knife, outline a well in the cake leaving a 3/4" thick wall around the hole, and along the outside. Leave at least 1" at the base. With a spoon, carefully dig out the cake from this area, saving 1 1/2 cups of cake chunks, which you crumble into smaller pieces.
Measure 2 1/2 cups of chocolate mousse and place in a small bowl, then fold in the cooled gelatin. Fill the well in the cake with this mixture and replace the top of the cake.
Mix 1/2 cup of chocolate mousse with the reserved crumbled cake, and fill in the hole in the center of the cake.
Frost the top and sides of the cake with the remaining mousse and refrigerate until chilled.
Serves 10 to 12.

CHOCOLATE SNOWBALLS

This is a must for chocolate lovers. The snowballs should be made a day in advance, since they have to "rest" in the refrigerator for at least 8 hours. They keep for several days.

10 ounces good semisweet or bittersweet chocolate
3/4 cup coffee
1 1/4 cup sugar
3/4 cup butter or pareve margarine, cut into pieces

5 large eggs
whipping cream or pareve cream substitute
confectioner's sugar to taste
1 Tablespoon dark rum - optional

Preheat oven to 350°F.
Melt the chocolate with the coffee slowly in a double boiler over simmering water.
In an electric mixer, mix the melted chocolate and the sugar until combined.
Piece by piece toss in the butter, mixing well.
Add the eggs, one at a time, beating well after each addition. Beat mixture for 2 minutes.
Pour mixture into a greased, deep (at least 3" to 4" deep), heavy glass or enamel baking dish.
Bake for an hour. Allow snowball mixture to cool, then refrigerate overnight, covered.
Scoop chocolate mixture with an ice cream scoop to form individual balls.
Cover each ball with whipped cream sweetened with powdered sugar and rum.
Makes 6 to 8 balls.

COLD OVEN POUND CAKE

1/2 pound butter
1/2 cup vegetable oil
3 cups sugar
5 large eggs
1 teaspoon vanilla

3 cups all purpose flour
1/2 teaspoon baking powder
1/4 teaspoon salt
1 cup milk

In a mixer, beat butter until well creamed. Scrape down the sides of the bowl and slowly add oil and sugar, alternately, and beating well. Add eggs one at a time, beating well after each addition. Add vanilla.
Mix together dry ingredients, and add them alternately with milk. Beat well.
Pour into greased and floured tube pan. Put cake in oven and THEN turn on oven to 350°F.
Bake for 1 1/4 hours.
Serves 12.

DATE NUT TORTE

6 large eggs, separated
1 1/2 cups sugar
12 ounces dates, coarsely chopped
1 1/2 cups chopped walnuts
1 1/2 tablespoons all purpose flour

1 tablespoon baking powder
2 cups whipping cream or pareve cream
  substitute
1 teaspoon vanilla
confectioner's sugar to taste

Preheat the oven to 350°F.
Grease and dust with flour two 8" or 9" round cake pans (preferably with removable bottoms).
In a large bowl with an electric mixer at medium speed, beat the egg yolks until thick and lemon colored, then slowly add the sugar in three parts, beating well after each addition.
With a wooden spoon, stir in the dates and walnuts.
Sift the flour and baking powder together and stir into the batter.
Wash and dry the beaters well and with the electric mixer at high speed beat the egg whites until stiff. Using a rubber spatula, gently fold the beaten egg whites into the batter; spoon the batter into the prepared pans and bake for 25 minutes.
Let the layers cool in their pans on a wire rack for 15 minutes then carefully remove the cakes from the pans and let them cool on a wire rack. At this point the layers can be frozen or refrigerated for later use.
About an hour before serving, in a large bowl with the electric mixer on high speed, whip the cream with the vanilla and confectioner's sugar to taste until stiff peaks form.
Spread the whipped cream between the layers and frost the top and sides of the torte with the remaining whipped cream, then place the torte in the refrigerator until serving.
Serves 8 to 10.

DECADENT AND QUICK

Company coming? Need a quick dessert? This can be prepared quickly with ingredients found in your cupboard. Can be made ahead or frozen (if freezing, don't ice with Cool Whip or whipped cream).

18 1/2 ounce chocolate Devil's Food cake mix
14 ounce can sweetened condensed milk

6 or 7 ounce jar caramel or fudge sauce
8 ounces Cool Whip or whipped cream

Prepare cake according to package directions, and bake in a 9" x 13" cake pan. As soon as cake tests done, remove from oven, let cool for 3 to 5 minutes, then prick warm cake all over the top with a toothpick or a fork. Pour the milk slowly over the top of the cake, letting the milk sink into the holes. Then slowly pour the caramel or fudge sauce over the top of the cake, pricking more holes if needed. If you pour too fast the milk and fudge will just flow off the top of the cake. Chill or freeze when cooled. Ice before serving.
Serves 8 to 12.

FUDGE ROLL

This was one of the most sought after recipes of Mrs. Kaplan, a famous Newton, Mass. caterer. Don't serve this unless you are willing to share the recipe with your friends!

6 large eggs, separated, and at room
  temperature
3/4 cup sugar
6 ounces semisweet chocolate chips

1/4 cup water
2 Tablespoons unsweetened cocoa
1 pint whipping cream or pareve substitute

Preheat oven to 350°F.

In a large bowl, with an electric mixer at medium speed, beat the egg yolks and sugar until thick and lemon colored - about 5 minutes.

In the top of a double boiler, over hot water, melt the chocolate with the water. Remove from heat and let cool. When chocolate has cooled to room temperature, add it to the egg yolk mixture.

Thoroughly wash the beaters and bowl, and with the mixer at low speed, beat the egg whites until bubbles begin to form. Turn mixer to high and continue beating until stiff.

Carefully, using a rubber spatula, fold the egg whites into the chocolate mixture.

Grease an 10 1/2" x15" jelly roll pan and line it with waxed paper. Grease and flour the waxed paper.

Spread the batter evenly around the pan and bake for 20 minutes. Do not overbake.

Remove the pan from the oven and cover the cake with a lightly dampened linen dishtowel.

Leave the cloth on the cake for 15 minutes (it will help draw out the heat so the cake will roll).

Place another lightly damp cloth on a flat surface and cover it with a piece of waxed paper that is 17" long. Sprinkle the cocoa evenly over the waxed paper.

Invert the cake onto the cocoa covered paper. Carefully peel off the waxed paper that the cake was baked with.

Carefully place the cake and cocoa covered waxed paper on a long platter or a cookie sheet covered in aluminum foil.

Whip the cream until soft peaks form. Spread 3/4 of the cream over the cake to within l" of all edges. Roll the cake up lengthwise, removing the waxed paper as you roll.

Ice the cake, if desired, with remaining cream. Refrigerate until serving.

Serves 10 to 12.

HINT: All ingredients for cakes and cookies should be at room temperature before you begin

GATEAU DE CREPES WITH APPLES

One of the most popular dessert in my cooking classes. It's sure to be an instant winner and become a holiday tradition with your family.

Crepes:

1 1/2 cups milk
1 1/2 cups all purpose flour
3 large eggs

1 Tablespoon sugar
1 teaspoon melted butter, cooled

Pour milk, flour, eggs, sugar, and melted butter into a blender or processor and blend until smooth. If possible, let batter sit at room temperature for two hours.
Heat a 7" or 8" crepe pan on medium heat for 3 to 5 minutes and then brush lightly with a little melted butter. Add just enough batter to barely cover the bottom of the pan.
Brown crepe lightly on one side, turn over and cook another minute or two.
Remove from pan and repeat process, buttering the pan as needed.
Makes about 20 crepes.

Filling:

2 Tablespoons butter
2 pounds tart apples, peeled, cored, and
  chopped

1 cup sugar
1/4 cup apple juice or Calvados
1 1/2 cups slivered almonds

Meringue:

2 large egg whites

1/4 cup sugar

Melt the butter in a large, heavy pot with a tight fitting lid. Add apples and toss to coat with butter, then cook, covered, over low heat, stirring occasionally until apples are soft - about 20 to 30 minutes.
Stir in sugar and apple juice or Calvados, and cook uncovered, stirring frequently for about 5 minutes over medium heat.
Spread about 2 to 3 TBL of apple mixture on a crepe, all the way to the edges.
Place this crepe on a buttered cookie sheet or 10" quiche dish.
Sprinkle 1 TBL almonds on the apples, place another crepe on top and repeat, using all crepes, apples, and nuts. Dessert may be made ahead up to this point. Refrigerate if making ahead.
Before serving preheat oven to 400°F.
In a mixing bowl with the mixer on low begin beating egg whites until foamy. Turn mixer to high and add the sugar, a TBL at a time, until you have a stiff meringue. Ice Gateau of Crepes with meringue as you would a cake. Bake for 5 to 7 minutes, or until meringue is lightly browned.
Serves 8 to 10.

JEWISH APPLE CAKE

This seems to be the recipe that I receive the most requests for. I once had a call from India from a student because she had lost her copy!

4 to 6 firm apples, peeled and sliced
2 teaspoon cinnamon
2 1/4 cups sugar
3 cups all purpose flour
1 Tablespoon baking powder

1 cup vegetable oil
4 large eggs
1/3 cup orange juice
1/2 teaspoon salt
2 1/2 teaspoons vanilla

Preheat the oven to 350°F, and grease and flour a 10" tube pan.
In a medium bowl, combine the apples with the cinnamon and 1/4 cup of the sugar - set aside.
In a large bowl, with an electric mixer at medium speed, combine the remaining sugar, the flour, baking powder, oil, eggs, orange juice, salt, and the vanilla. Beat just until the batter is smooth.
Pour a small amount of the batter into the prepared pan, and place a layer of the apple slices on top. Continue layering in this fashion, ending with a layer of batter.
Bake for 1 1/2 hours, or until cake tests done.
Cool the cake in its pan for 30 minutes on a wire rack; then turn the cake out onto the rack to cool.
Serves 12.

HINT: Place an apple cut in half in a cake container to keep cake fresh.

IRRESISTIBLE BROWNIES

4 oz unsweetened chocolate, chopped
1 cup butter
4 large eggs
2 cups sugar
1/4 teaspoon salt
1 cup flour
1 teaspoon vanilla
1/2 cup melted butter or margarine

1 lb confectioners' sugar
1/4 cup whipping cream
1 cup chopped nuts
1/4 cup dry white sherry
6 oz semi sweet chocolate
4 tablespoons butter or margarine
3 tablespoons water

Preheat oven to 325F. Grease a 9x13-inch baking pan.
Carefully melt unsweetened chocolate, and stir in 1 cup butter until it is melted.
Beat the eggs in a mixer and add the sugar and salt. Stir in the cooled chocolate, mix well and add the flour and vanilla.
Pour into prepared baking pan. Bake for 30 to 40 minutes. Remove from oven and cool.
With a mixer beat together butter, sugar, and cream. Add the nuts and sherry and mix well. Spread over cooled chocolate layer. Chill.
In a small pan, melt the semi sweet chocolate with 4 tablespoons butter or margarine and water. Spread over iced cookies and chill until firm. Freezes well.
Makes about 24.

KEY LIME TORTE

A beautiful low fat dessert to serve for any occasion.

Cake:

1 package lite yellow cake mix
2 Tablespoons lime juice plus enough water to equal 1 cup

1/2 cup lite butter or margarine, softened
4 large egg whites

Filling:

14 ounce can low fat sweetened condensed milk
1/2 cup lime juice

2 cups lite frozen topping (like Cool Whip)

Preheat oven to 350°F. Spray two 8" or 9" round cake pans.
In a large bowl, combine all cake ingredients at low speed until moistened.
Beat 2 minutes at high speed and pour batter into prepared pans.
Bake for 20 to 30 minutes. Cool on a wire rack for at least 15 minutes and remove from pans.
Cool completely.
In a small bowl, combine the sweetened condensed milk and 1/2 cup lime juice, mixing well.
In a large bowl fold 1 cup frozen topping into the condensed milk.
To assemble cake, slice each layer in half horizontally to make 4 layers.
Place one layer cut side up on a serving plate and spread with 1/3 of the frozen topping mixture.
Top with remaining cake and repeat. Spread reserved frozen topping on top of torte.
Refrigerate 2 to 3 hours before serving and garnish with lime slices.
Serves 10 to 12.

MELT IN YOUR MOUTH CHOCOLATE DELIGHT

A marvelous, simple chocolate confection.

3 (one ounce each) squares unsweetened
   chocolate
1/4 cup water
6 Tablespoons butter or pareve margarine
3 large eggs, separated and at room
   temperature

1 teaspoon vanilla
3/4 cup sugar
1/4 cup all purpose flour
optional: whipped topping and/or hot fudge
   or chocolate sauce

Preheat oven to 375°F.
In the top of a double boiler, over gently simmering water, combine chocolate, water and butter.
Stir and heat until chocolate and butter are melted. Pour into a large mixing bowl and beat, adding
egg yokes one at a time. Beat well after each addition.
Add vanilla and sugar and continue beating for another three minutes or until well mixed.
Add flour, beat until blended.
Thoroughly wash and dry beaters and mixing bowl and beat egg whites until stiff then fold egg
whites into chocolate mixture.
Butter or grease a 4 cup ring mold and carefully pour in batter.
Place ring mold into a larger baking pan and fill baking pan with enough hot water to come half
way up the outside of the ring mold. Bake for 40 minutes.
Remove ring mold from water bath and cool on a wire rack for 5 to 10 minutes.
Unmold onto a serving platter and cool to room temperature.
Cut into thin slices and serve with whipped topping, hot fudge or chocolate sauce.
Serves 8 to 10.

PASSOVER STRAWBERRY TORTE

A friend brought this to my house last Passover and everyone wanted the recipe. This is so good you will want to use it all year round. It is also low in calories and goes from freezer to table.

Macaroon Nut Crust:

5 ounces (about 1 1/2 cups) almond macaroons
2 Tablespoons unsalted butter or margarine, melted

1/2 cup chopped pecans or walnuts

Filling:

2 large egg whites, at room temperature
1 cup sugar
2 cups sliced strawberries

2 Tablespoons lemon juice
1 teaspoon vanilla

Strawberry Sauce:

10 ounce package frozen sliced strawberries
3 Tablespoons frozen undiluted orange juice concentrate or 2 TBL orange marmalade

1 Tablespoons currant jelly
1 cup fresh strawberries, sliced

Preheat oven to 350°F.

Prepare crust by placing macaroons and butter in a food processor with the steel blade and process until coarsely ground. Add nuts and process until mixture begins to hold together.

Press mixture onto the bottom of a 10" spring form pan. Bake for 5 to 10 minutes or until golden. Remove from oven and cool.

In a large bowl of a mixer, place the egg whites, sugar, 2 cups of sliced strawberries, lemon juice and vanilla. Beat on low speed to blend, then increase speed to high and beat until firm peaks form when beaters are removed - about 10 minutes. Pour into cooled crust.

Cover and freeze until very firm, a minimum of 6 hours or overnight. At this point it may be frozen for 3 weeks. Before serving, prepare strawberry sauce, which can be made the day before. Slightly defrost strawberries and orange juice concentrate. Puree strawberries with concentrate or marmalade in food processor with the metal blade. Mix in currant jelly.

Remove bowl and stir in sliced strawberries. Serve sauce with torte.

Serve torte directly from freezer, as it will not be totally solid.

Serves 10.

HINT: Never use stale walnuts in a recipe since they will ruin it, especially if the oil in the nuts has become rancid. Keep nuts fresh by storing them in the freezer.

PAT TABIBIAN'S FABULOUS APPLE "CAKE"

6 ounce package vanilla wafer - type cookies, finely crushed
2 Tablespoons sugar
l teaspoon ground cinnamon
4 Tablespoons unsalted butter, melted and cooled
2 Tablespoons unsalted butter

6 to 8 Golden Delicious apples, peeled, cored, and thinly sliced
2/3 cup sugar
1 1/2 Tablespoons cornstarch dissolved in 1 1/2 Tablespoons cold water
6 large eggs, room temperature
2 cups sour cream
2 teaspoons vanilla

Prepare crust by combining cookies, 2 TBL sugar, cinnamon, and 4 TBL melted butter.
Press evenly over bottom and sides of a 9" spring form pan, or a 9" x 13" baking pan.
Place the crust in the refrigerator while preparing filling. Preheat oven to 325°F.
Melt the butter in a large skillet and add the apple slices and sugar.
Cover and cook the apples over medium heat for about l0 minutes, or until apples begin to soften.
Stir the cornstarch/water mixture again and pour into the apples, stirring gently.
Continue cooking over low heat, stirring gently, until mixture thickens.
Remove the pan from the heat and allow to cool slightly.
Beat the eggs, sour cream, and vanilla together. Stir apples into this mixture and mix thoroughly.
Spoon mixture carefully over the prepared crust. Smooth the top.
Bake for approximately 45 minutes or until the center of the cake jiggles slightly but looks set when the pan is gently shaken. Cool and chill overnight before serving. Cooled cake freezes well.
Serves 10 to 12.

HINT: Eggs should never be added to ingredients that are hot (unless specifically stated in the recipe) because they will curdle.

PINEAPPLE POUND CAKE

1/2 cup vegetable shortening
1 cup butter or margarine, softened
2 3/4 cups sugar
6 large eggs
3 cups all purpose flour

1 teaspoon baking powder
1/4 cup milk mixed with 1 teaspoon vanilla
15 ounce can crushed pineapple
1/4 cup melted butter or margarine
1 1/2 cups sifted confectioner's sugar

In a large bowl, with the electric mixer at medium speed, cream the shortening, butter and sugar until mixture is light and fluffy then add the eggs one at a time, beating well after each addition. Combine the flour and baking powder and add it to the egg mixture alternately with the milk mixture. Stir well with a wooden spoon after each addition, or mix on the lowest speed.
Measure 3/4 cup of crushed pineapple along with a few tablespoons of the juice from the can and add it to the batter.
Drain the juice from the remaining pineapple, discard it, and set aside the pineapple for the glaze.
Pour the batter into a well greased 10" tube or bundt pan and place the cake in a cold oven.
Set the oven temperature to 325°F and bake the cake for 1 1/4 hours or until the cake tests done.
Cool the cake in its pan on a wire rack for 30 minutes, then invert the cake onto a serving plate.
While cake is cooling, combine the melted butter or margarine with the sugar, mixing till smooth. Stir in the remaining pineapple, and drizzle the mixture over the top and sides of the cake when the cake is cool.
Serves 16 to 20.

HINT: To store fresh pineapple properly, don't subject it to temperature changes. If it was chilled when you bought it at the store, keep it chilled at home. If the store had it at room temperature, keep it at room temperature. This prevents the pineapple from developing dark spots, which result from temperature changes.

GREEK WALNUT SPICE CAKE

The combination of nuts, a moist cake, and a syrupy bottom will have your guests begging for the recipe. Ellen, a friend I met while teaching at Jungle Jim's in Cincinnati shared this family recipe with me.

Canola spray for greasing
1 cup Canola oil
1 1/2 cups sugar
3 large eggs
1 cup milk with 1 teaspoon vinegar
   mixed in

3 teaspoons baking powder
1/2 teaspoon baking soda
1 teaspoon cinnamon
1/2 teaspoon ground cloves
2 cups flour
1 cup chopped walnuts

Syrup
2 cups sugar
1 cup water

2 sticks cinnamon
1 teaspoon fresh lemon juice

Preheat oven to 350F. Grease and flour a 9x13-inch baking pan.
In a mixer at medium speed, beat together oil and sugar, for about 3 minutes until well mixed.
Add eggs, one at a time, beating well after each addition.
Add baking powder, baking soda, cinnamon, and cloves, mixing well.
On lowest speed of mixer add flour and milk alternately.
Stir in nuts and pour batter into prepared pan. Bake for about 35 to 40 minutes or until a toothpick inserted in the center comes out clean. Cool in pan on a wire rack. Cut into diamond shapes.
Prepare syrup. Combine all ingredients in a saucepan and bring to a boil. Boil on medium heat for 5 to 7 minutes, stirring constantly. Pour hot syrup over cooled cake.
Let cake sit for several hours so all the syrup is absorbed well. Remove and put in cupcake papers if desired.
Serves 12.

HINT: Use pans that are 2 to 3-inches deep. In pans that are shallower, the cake bakes up to the top of the pan but then continues to rise into a "bump" or "crown" in the middle.

RASPBERRY WHITE CHOCOLATE CHEESECAKE

2 cups crumbs made from vanilla wafer type
   cookies
1/2 cup butter, melted
32 ounces cream cheese, softened to room
   temperature
1 1/2 cups sugar

4 large eggs
2 Tablespoons all purpose flour
1 1/2 teaspoons vanilla
1/4 teaspoon almond extract
8 ounces white chocolate, melted
2 cups fresh raspberries

Preheat oven to 350°F. Mix crumbs and butter and press into 10" springform pan.
Beat cream cheese until fluffy, then beat in sugar and add eggs one at a time.
Gradually stir in flour, vanilla, and almond extract. Slowly add melted chocolate and beat until combined. Sprinkle berries over crust. Pour cheesecake mixture on top.
Place in preheated oven and immediately turn oven down to 250°F.
Bake for 1 3/4 to 2 hours or until cheesecake is set in the middle. Let cool and refrigerate overnight.
Serves 10 to 12.

SINFULLY DELICIOUS KAHLUA CAKE

This cake can be served as a layered cake or a trifle.

1 chocolate cake made from your
favorite recipe or a mix
1/4 cup Kahlua
5 ounce box chocolate pudding, instant or
   regular, prepared according to directions

12 ounce container frozen topping (such as
   CoolWhip)
3 to 4 large Heath's Butterfingers candy bars,
   coarsely chopped in a blender or processor

Cut the cake horizontally into 3 or 4 layers, or tear into pieces for trifle. On a cake plate (or in a large brandy snifter) place one layer of the cake.
Sprinkle with 1/3 or 1/4 of the Kahlua (depending on whether you have 3 or 4 layers).
Spread with 1/3 or 1/4 of the chocolate pudding.
Top with 1/3 or 1/4 of the CoolWhip. Sprinkle with 1/3 or 1/4 of the candy.
Repeat, using all the ingredients. End with the CoolWhip (ice the cake or spread on top the trifle).
Sprinkle with remaining candy.
Serves 8 to 10.

TEXAS CAKE IN A POT

3 heaping Tablespoons cocoa powder
1/4 pound of butter or margarine
1/2 cup vegetable oil
1 cup water
2 cups sugar
2 cups all purpose flour
1/2 cup buttermilk
2 large eggs

1 teaspoon baking soda
1 teaspoon cinnamon
1 teaspoon vanilla
1 stick butter or margarine
4 heaping Tablespoons cocoa powder
6 Tablespoons milk (more if needed)
1 pound box confectioner's sugar
chopped walnuts - optional

Preheat oven to 400°F.
In a saucepan combine the cocoa, butter, oil and water. Bring to a boil and remove pot from heat.
Sift together the sugar and flour. Pour over the cocoa mixture and beat until smooth. Combine buttermilk, eggs, baking soda, cinnamon, and vanilla and beat into the above mixture.
Grease and flour a 10" x 15" baking pan and pour in batter. Bake for 20 to 30 minutes or until cake tests done.
Combine butter, cocoa, milk in a pan and heat to boiling. Remove from heat and stir in the confectioner's sugar and beat until thick. If more milk is needed, add a little at a time and mix well. Frost the hot cake and top with chopped nuts if desired.
Serves 8.

HINT: A FEW ESSENTIALS FOR BAKING A CAKE:
Use metal pans 2 to 3" deep. In shallower pans the cake bakes up to the top of the pan well, then continues to rise into a "crown" in the middle. Fill pan 2/3 full. When pan is placed in the oven the first thing to heat up is the pan, affecting the way the cake bakes - even or uneven. For a more uniform cake, push the batter up the sides of the pan and into the corners of square pans before baking. This coating helps the rest of the batter to crawl up the pan easier, contributing to a more even layer.

When greasing and flouring the pan be careful not to over-flour since it will only create more crumbs. Use the grease/flour spray.

Use only large eggs at room temperature (allows more egg white to release from the shell) yielding a lighter, fluffier batter.

Scrape the sides of the bowl often during mixing for a more uniform batter.

Lower the oven tempeature about 25° when baking a cake. 325°F is a good standard temperature. This assists in letting the entire cake bake and rise at a more consistent rate by not allowing the batter touching the sides of the pan to bake too quickly. It may take 5 to 10 minutes longer to bake.

Test for doneness by inserting a cake tester in the center - it should come out clean; lightly touch the top and if it springs back it is usually done, or if the cake begins to pull away from the sides of the pan it is close to being done.

Cool the cake on a wire rack. This allows air to flow underneath the cake and cool it faster without the bottom becoming "gummy."

THE ULTIMATE CHOCOLATE CAKE

The name says it all! For Passover I just omit the flour.

4 bars (4 ounces each) German Sweet
   Chocolate
1/2 cup unsalted butter or pareve margarine,
   softened to room temperature

4 large eggs, separated
4 teaspoons sugar
4 teaspoons all purpose flour

Preheat oven to 425°F. and grease a 9"x 5"x 3" loaf pan. Line with waxed paper.
In the top of a double boiler, melt the chocolate over hot but not boiling water, stirring occasionally. Remove from the heat and vigorously stir in the butter. Let mixture cool.
With an electric mixer at high speed, beat the egg whites until stiff peaks form. Set aside.
In another bowl, beat the egg yolks at medium speed, and gradually add the sugar.
Beat until thick and lemon colored - about 5 to 8 minutes.
Add the flour but just beat until blended. Stir in the cooled chocolate mixture.
With a rubber spatula carefully fold in the egg whites, making sure everything is thoroughly incorporated (batter should be one color).
Pour the mixture into the prepared pan, reduce the oven temperature to 350°F and bake for 25 to 30 minutes. Cool cake pan on a wire rack. The cake will "collapse" - don't panic!
When cool refrigerate the cake in its pan for several hours.
To serve, loosen the cake by running a metal spatula around the edge of the pan.
Invert the cake onto a serving platter and carefully peel off waxed paper.
I like to serve it at room temperature - some like to serve it right from the refrigerator - the taste will be different!
Serves 12 to 16 if cut into 1/2" slices (it is very rich).

HINT: Melting chocolate is tricky – if you don't handle it properly it will burn, seize up, or lump with seemingly no provocation. For success, chop it finely then place in a double boiler over a gently simmering water. Stir, and do not let any water or steam get on the chocolate.

WHITE CHOCOLATE MOUSSE BOMBE

This is from Judy Kancigor's family cookbook, MELTING POT MEMORIES. It's a very light cheesecake. Don't be afraid to use the plastic wrap - it doesn't burn!

5 ounces white chocolate
2 pounds cream cheese
1 1/2 cups sugar

3 whole large eggs
2 large eggs, separated
1/2 teaspoon vanilla

Raspberry Coulis:

1 package frozen raspberries, in heavy syrup, thawed

1 Tablespoon lemon juice
1 Tablespoon kirsch

Preheat oven to 350°F. Melt white chocolate in double boiler.
Mix cream cheese and sugar in food processor until smooth and slowly pour melted chocolate into cream cheese mixture. Add eggs and yolks one at a time with vanilla through feed tube while processor is on.
Beat whites lightly with mixer (not stiff) and fold in. Pour into stainless steel bowl lined (crisscrossed) with plastic wrap and cover well with plastic wrap, then set the bowl in larger bowl with hot water (big enough so you can get smaller bowl out later) and cover tightly with foil. Bake 2 hours or until center no longer jiggles.
Invert on plate and remove bowl and cool for 2 to 3 hours.
Prepare the raspberry coulis by pureeing raspberries, lemon juice, and kirsch until smooth in your processor or blender. Serve with bombe.
 Serves 6 to 8.

COOKIES

CHOCOLATE ROSES

2 (7 ounce each) milk or dark chocolate Hershey bars
2 ounces (or 2 squares) unsweetened chocolate

4 to 6 cups corn flakes

In a microwave-safe dish, melt the chocolates together in the microwave.
Place the corn flakes in a large bowl and pour in the melted chocolate, tossing to coat the corn flakes. Scoop out with an ice cream scoop and place on a cookie sheet sprayed with Pam. Freeze for 10 to 20 minutes. Store in the freezer until ready to serve, and bring to room temperature.
Makes about 12 or more "flowers."

NANAIMO BARS

First had these at my cousins in Minneapolis many many many years ago, then in Alaska and Canada. They are very addictive and I could eat the whole pan.

Bottom layer:
2 cups graham cracker crumbs or
   1 1/ 2 cups ground chocolate cookie
   crumbs
1 cup sweetened coconut flakes
1/ 2 cup chopped walnuts
8 tablespoons unsalted butter, at room
   temperature, cut into small pieces
6 tablespoons unsweetened cocoa powder
1/ 4 cup sugar
1 large egg, lightly beaten

Middle layer:
2 cups confectioners' sugar
3 tablespoons cream
4 tablespoons unsalted butter, melted
1/ 2 teaspoon vanilla
grated zest of a small or medium lemon

Top layer:
6 ounces semisweet chocolate chips
1 tablespoon unsalted butter

Preheat oven to 350F. Generously butter a 9-inch square metal baking pan and set aside.
Prepare the bottom layer: Toss the crumbs, coconut, and walnuts together in a large bowl. Place in prepared baking pan.
In a small, heavy, pan over low heat, combine butter, cocoa powder, sugar, and egg, stirring until the butter has melted and the mixture is smooth and well mixed (about 3 minutes).
Pour the butter/cocoa mixture on top of the crumb mixture in the pan, and using a fork, mix them together until crumb mixture is thoroughly moistened.
With your fingers, press the crumb mixture evenly over the bottom of the pan. Bake until the layer is just firm to the touch, 10 to 12 minutes.
Remove pan from oven and let the bottom layer cool completely.
Prepare the middle layer: Mix the sugar, cream, butter, vanilla, and lemon zest together in a mixing bowl until it is smooth and icing-like. If it needs to be a little more spreadable, add a little more cream.
Spread this icing over the cooled baked layer in the pan. Refrigerate until the icing is firm, about 30 minutes or more.
Prepare the top layer: Melt the chocolate and butter together in the top of a double boiler placed over simmering water. Stir until the mixture is smooth and shiny, about 3 to 4 minutes. Let it cool for a minute or two, then spread it evenly with an icing spatula over the icing layer. Refrigerate just until the chocolate sets, about 15 minutes.
Cut into 16 large or 32 small squares. Make sure you cut the squares while the chocolate is firm but not hard or it will crack when cut.
These can be made 3 to 4 days ahead and refrigerated or made ahead, covered well, and frozen.
Makes 16 or 32 squares.

DECADENT CHOCOLATE HEAVEN

1 pound imported bittersweet chocolate, finely chopped
1 cup unsalted butter, cut into tablespoons
1/3 cup strong brewed coffee

4 large eggs, at room temperature
1 1/2 cups granulated sugar
1/2 cup all purpose flour
8 ounces pecans, coarsely chopped - about 2 cups

Preheat oven to 375°F. Line 9" x 13" pan with double thickness of foil so that it extends 2" beyond the sides. Grease the bottom and sides of foil lined pan.
In the top of a double boiler, melt chocolate over simmering water. Stir in the butter and coffee, stirring frequently until mixture is smooth. Remove chocolate from the heat and cool, stirring occasionally. Let sit for 10 minutes.
In a mixer, beat the eggs on high speed for 30 seconds or until foamy.
Gradually add sugar and continue to beat for 2 minutes until eggs are light and fluffy.
Reduce mixer to low speed and gradually beat in the cooled chocolate mixture.
Using a wooden spoon, stir in the flour and nuts. Do not over beat the mixture.
Pour the batter into prepared pan and spread evenly. Bake for 28 to 30 minutes or until the cookies are set around the edges. They will remain moist in the center.
Cool the cookies in the pan on a wire rack for 30 minutes.
Cover the pan tightly with aluminum foil and refrigerate overnight. Remove the top foil and run a sharp knife around the edge of the cookies. Lift the cookies out of the pan, inverting onto a large plate. Peel off the foil and invert again onto a smooth surface. Cut in squares and serve.
Makes about 24 cookies.

LIESEL'S RUGELACH

Pastry:
12 ounces cream cheese, at room temperature
16 ounces unsalted butter, at room temperature

4 cups flour
1/ 2 teaspoon salt

Filling:
1 1/ 2 cups ground Macadamia nuts (or almonds or walnuts)
1 cup grated or shredded coconut
1/ 2 cup sugar

1 egg white
1 teaspoon vanilla
1 teaspoon almond extract

Egg wash: 1 egg mixed with 1 teaspoon of water

In the bowl of an electric mixer combine the cream cheese and butter until light and fluffy.
Turn speed to low and slowly add the flour and salt, mixing just until the mixture forms dough.
Place the ball of dough on a lightly floured surface and knead about 8 times. Divide dough into 4

(continued on next page)

pieces, (press each into a thick disk), wrap in plastic wrap, and refrigerate for at least 4 hours. The dough will keep for 2 weeks in the refrigerator or up to 3 months in the freezer (thaw in refrigerator overnight before using). Preheat oven to 350°F.

In the food processor, combine the nuts, coconut, egg white, sugar, vanilla, and almond extract. On a lightly floured surface, roll out each disk, one at a time, into a large thin circle. Spread 1/4 th of the filling onto the top of each circle, and press gently into the dough. Cut each circle into wedges (like a pizza) and each wedge into smaller wedges until the base of each wedge is about 1-1/2" inches wide. Carefully roll up each wedge starting from the wider end. Place on a lightly greased cookie sheet, brush with egg wash, and sprinkle with a little sugar. Chill in the refrigerator for 20 to 30 minutes. Bake for about 30 minutes or until lightly golden. Rugelach can be frozen unbaked and then baked frozen.

Makes between 2 to 3 dozen.

INDULGE YOURSELF CHEESECAKE BROWNIES

Cheese mixture:

1 teaspoon vanilla
2/3 cup sugar

2 large eggs
1 pound cream cheese, room temperature

Brownie mixture:

2 1/2 cups sugar
4 large eggs
1 cup unsalted butter, melted, cooled
1 1/2 cups all purpose flour

1/2 cup cocoa
1/2 teaspoon salt
2 teaspoons vanilla

Icing:

4 tablespoons unsalted butter, room
   temperature
3 cups confectioners' sugar, sifted

3 tablespoons cocoa
1 teaspoon vanilla
3 tablespoons cream or milk, more if needed

Preheat oven to 350°F. Grease a 9" x 13" baking pan.

In mixing bowl combine the ingredients for the cheese mixture and set aside. Combine the sugar and eggs for the brownie mixture in another bowl. Add the melted butter, then add the flour, cocoa, salt, and vanilla, mix well. Pour all the brownie mix into prepared pan, top with cream cheese mixture. Lightly swirl the 2 together, but do not mix. Bake 45 to 55 minutes or until toothpick comes out clean. Cool on a wire rack. For frosting, combine butter, sugar, and cocoa. Add the vanilla and 3 tablespoons cream, adding more as needed to spreading consistency. Remove the brownies from the pan before icing. Ice, let the icing set, then cut into neat squares. Store in refrigerator or freeze. Brownies are great by themselves, just bake them 30 to 35 minutes. Makes about 16 to 20 brownies.

MRS. KAPLAN'S NEVER TO BE FORGOTTEN MANDEL BREAD

I usually don't care for mandel bread because it isn't sweet enough for me, but I love this version.

1/2 cup vegetable shortening
l cup sugar
3 large eggs
3 cups all purpose flour
2 teaspoons baking powder
pinch of salt
1 teaspoon vanilla

l teaspoon almond extract
1/2 cup each of red and green maraschino
    cherries, cut up
1/2 cup or more golden raisins
6 ounces butterscotch morsels
1/2 cup chopped walnuts or almonds - optional

Icing:

1/2 cup sifted confectioner's sugar
1 teaspoon vanilla

1 Tablespoon butter, softened
1 to 2 Tablespoons warm milk

Preheat the oven to 350°F. In a large bowl, with an electric mixer at medium speed, cream the shortening and sugar. Add the eggs, one at a time, beating well after each addition.
Sift together the flour, baking powder, and the salt; using a wooden spoon, slowly add the flour mixture to the bowl. Stir in the vanilla, almond extract, cherries, raisins, butterscotch morsels, and the optional nuts. Form the dough into 3 strips, each about 12" long and 2" wide, and place all 3 on a large greased and floured cookie sheet. Bake for 20 to 25 minutes, then cool the strips on a wire rack.
Prepare the icing by combining the sugar, vanilla, and butter with enough warm milk to form a fairly liquid mixture. Pour the icing over the cooled strips and cut each strip into twelve l" slices. Makes 3 dozen cookies.

MARILYN SCHNAIR'S BEVERLY HILLS MANDEL BREAD

I met Marilyn and her husband on a cruise as they nibbled what looked like something great to eat. I asked for a piece, and fell in love with this unusual recipe.

3 large eggs
3/4 cup vegetable oil
1 cup sugar
3 cups all purpose flour
1 teaspoon baking powder
1 teaspoon vanilla
1 teaspoon water
1 teaspoon orange juice

1 teaspoon orange extract
1 teaspoon almond extract
1 teaspoon lemon extract
1 cup toasted chopped walnuts
1 cup chocolate chips
zest of one lemon
zest of one orange
cinnamon mixed with sugar.

Preheat oven to 350°F. All ingredients must be mixed together by HAND. (Marilyn wears "doctor's gloves" that she gets at the drug store). Grease a cookie sheet and place dough on it in 3 "loaves". Bake for 45 minutes in the center of the oven.
Remove from oven, sprinkle with cinnamon and sugar, turn and sprinkle the other side.
Slice in 1/2" slices. Return to the oven and bake another 5 minutes.
Makes about 3 to 4 dozen, depending on size.

HINT: To enhance the flavor intensity of your cookies, cream the vanilla into the butter or shortening and sugar first. This encapsulates the vanilla and helps prevent flavor loss. Never use artificial vanilla, as it may break down when products are frozen and not taste as good.

O HENRY BARS

2/3 cup butter (10 1/2 TBL) or margarine
1 cup dark brown sugar
3 teaspoons vanilla
1/2 cup lite corn syrup

4 cups quick oats
6 ounces semi sweet chocolate chips
2/3 cup chunky peanut butter

Preheat oven to 350°F. Butter a 9" x 13" baking pan.
Cream together the butter and sugar. Add the vanilla and corn syrup. Mix well.
Add quick oats and mix just until a dough forms. Pat dough into prepared pan.
Bake for 15 to 16 minutes.
In a small pan over medium heat, melt the chocolate and the peanut butter, and spread over dough once it has cooled.
Makes about 24 cookies.

SNAPPY GINGERSNAPS

3/4 cup shortening
1 cup sugar
1 large egg
1/4 cup molasses
2 cups all purpose flour
2 teaspoons baking soda

1 teaspoon cinnamon
3/4 teaspoon ginger
1/2 teaspoon cloves
1/4 teaspoon salt
mixture of cinnamon and sugar

Preheat oven to 375°F. Place everything in food processor except cinnamon and sugar and pulse to form dough. Pinch off pieces of dough and roll into mixture of sugar and cinnamon. Place on cookie sheet...leave space in between as they spread. Bake for 8 minutes, longer if you like them crispy. Makes 2 to 3 dozen cookies.

SWEET ROUNDS WITH ALMONDS

These "Turkish Delights" are from my friend Ali, a fabulous chef.

Syrup:
2 cups sugar
1 cup water
slice of lemon

Cookies:

2 sticks plus 2 Tablespoons butter
2 large eggs
4 cups (or more) flour
3/ 4 cup plus 1 tablespoon sugar

1 heaping teaspoon baking powder
zest of one orange
1 teaspoon vanilla - optional
60 whole blanched almonds

Boil sugar and water, stirring, for about 3 to 4 minutes, reduce heat and simmer for 10 minutes, then add lemon, stir, cook a minute and remove from the heat. Pour into bowl. Let cool.
Preheat oven to 350°F. Place oven shelf in upper 1/3 of oven.
In a large bowl, combine with your hands the softened butter, eggs, flour, sugar, baking powder and zest. Work dough with fingers until a ball of dough is formed.
Break off a pieces of dough and roll between your palms, or on a work surface, to form a log. Place on a cutting board and cut into 1" pieces. Roll each piece between palms and slap onto ungreased jelly roll pan. Gently slightly flatten each ball, and place on the pan. Make an indenture with your thumb in each cookie and stick a nut in each one. Continue until all the dough is used up.
Bake about 12 to 14 minutes, then check the bottoms of each cookie. They should be lightly golden and the tops light brown. Break one in half to see if the insides are baked, if not continue to bake, but watch carefully so the bottoms do not burn.. Remove from oven and pour syrup over cookies. After a few minutes turn the cookies over so other side is in syrup. (If nuts fall out, just stick them back when you turn them over again. Makes about 50 cookies.

APPLE WALNUT PIE

Crust:

1 1/2 cups all purpose flour
salt

dash sugar
1 stick butter or margarine cut into pieces

Filling:

6 to 7 Rome, Beauty or other apples, sliced by hand
1 1/4 cups sour cream or a sour cream substitute

1/2 cup all purpose flour
1 large egg
3/4 cup sugar
1 teaspoon vanilla

Topping:

1/4 cup brown sugar
1/4 cup white sugar
1/2 cup all purpose flour

3/4 stick butter or margarine
2 cups chopped walnuts

Preheat oven to 350°F.

Place flour, salt, sugar, and butter into a food processor and add enough ice water to bind and make dough. Flatten the ball of dough, chill, rollout and place in 9" or 10" pie pan.

Flute edges and refrigerate until dough chills.

Prepare filling by mixing all filling ingredients together in a large bowl. Let mixture sit for 10 minutes and pour into pie shell. Mix topping ingredients together and pour over filling.

Bake for and hour to an hour and fifteen minutes.

While baking, cover the walnuts with foil for 1/2 of the cooking time.

When pie is done, remove from oven and cool on a wire rack. Do not serve or cut for 24 hours.

Serve at room temperature.

Serves 8.

BEST AND MOST UNUSUAL LEMON PIE EVER

One minute it's sweet, one minute it's tart but it's a sure winner any time.

2 large lemons, very thinly sliced with the
   peel on
2 cups sugar

4 large eggs
1 box pie crusts with 2 crusts or 2 home made
   pie crusts

Preheat oven to 425°F.
Slice the lemon "circles" in half (so they look like half moons), and remove any seeds.
Place the lemons in a large bowl and cover with the sugar. Let this mixture sit for 2 hours at room temperature.
Place one crust in the bottom of a 9" pie pan.
Beat the eggs well and mix with the lemon sugar mixture, mixing well.
Pour the mixture into the crust and cover with the remaining crust, pinching edges together.
With a sharp knife, make several slits in the top crust to allow steam to escape during baking.
Bake for 15 minutes. Lower the oven temperature to 350°F and bake another 35 to 40 minutes, or until the crust is golden brown. Cool the pie on a wire rack for 30 minutes.
Chill thoroughly before serving, or freeze.
Serves 6 to 8.

HINT: Citrus fruits yield nearly twice the amount of juice if they are dropped into hot water for a few minutes before you squeeze them, or roll them back and forth beneath your hand on the counter top first.

CRAZY CRUST PIE

A great recipe for those who love pies but who hate to make pie crusts - or, like me, eat the inside and discard the crust! In the summer I use peaches instead of apples.

5 to 6 large apples, peeled, cored, and sliced
   (or peaches)
4 Tablespoons sugar
1 1/2 teaspoons cinnamon

4 Tablespoons butter or margarine
1 cup sugar
2 large eggs
1 cup all purpose flour

Preheat oven to 350°F. Place the apple slices in a 9" or 10" pie pan.
Combine the sugar and cinnamon and sprinkle half over the apples.
In a medium bowl with an electric mixer at medium speed, cream together the margarine and the sugar. Add the eggs, one at a time, beating well after each addition.
Add the flour, mixing only until ingredients are blended.
Spread the batter over the fruit, being careful to leave a 1" rim of fruit showing at the edge.
Sprinkle the remaining sugar-cinnamon mixture over the batter.
Bake the pie for one hour. Cool on a wire rack for one hour.
Serve the pie at room temperature or chilled. Freezes beautifully.
Serves 6 to 8.

CHOCOLATE PEANUT BUTTER CREAM CHEESE PIE

Prepare this winner a day before serving. As long as I am getting out the mixer, I always double the recipe and have one to freeze. This can be made for Passover using adjustments.*

3/4 cup sugar
8 ounces cream cheese, softened
1/4 cup sour cream
1 1/4 teaspoons fresh lemon juice

2 large eggs
6 Tablespoons creamy peanut butter
1/2 cup semi sweet chocolate chips
9" graham cracker or chocolate crumb pie crust

Frosting:

1/2 cup semi sweet chocolate chips
1/4 cup sugar

1/4 cup sour cream

Preheat oven to 350°F.
In a medium bowl, with the mixer on medium, combine sugar, cream cheese, sour cream, lemon juice, eggs and peanut butter. Fold in the chocolate chips and pour the mixture into a pie shell.
Bake for 35 minutes. Remove from the oven and cool 15 minutes. Leave the oven on.
In a small saucepan, melt the chocolate chips, sugar and sour cream.
Spread over pie. Bake for 10 minutes. Cool, cover and refrigerate overnight.
Serves 6 to 8.

*For Passover, buy a kosher for Passover ready- made piecrust. Instead of peanut butter, grind together 4 teaspoons of canola oil and 1/2 cup roasted cashew nuts. Rest of recipe stays the same.

VERY BERRY PIE

This is so simple and quick, but it's eaten just as quickly.

1 quart strawberries, blueberries, blackberries
   or raspberries, or a mixture of any of these
2 ready made or home made graham cracker
   pie crusts
1 1/2 cups water

2 Tablespoons cornstarch
3/4 cup sugar
3 ounce box "matching" fruit" jello (strawberry
   flavor for strawberries, etc.)

Place berries carefully in the pie shells. In a pot over medium heat, combine the water, cornstarch and sugar. Cook, stirring, until clear, and sugar is dissolved.
Stir in jello and continue cooking another minute or two, until it is dissolved.
Pour the glaze over the fruit and let cool. Cover and refrigerate overnight.
Served with whipped topping if desired.
Serves 6.

HINT: When using fresh berries, freeze them first for 1 1/2 hours so they won't "bleed."

DELECTABLE OTHERS

BANANAS FOSTER A LA MEXICO

4 Tablespoons butter or margarine	juice of 2 oranges
4 large cooking bananas, peeled and sliced in half lengthwise	grated rind (zest) of one orange
	1/2 cup regular or low fat sour cream
1 cup dark brown sugar	1/2 cup confectioner's sugar

In a large skillet over low heat, slowly melt the butter being careful not to let it brown or burn.
Fry the halves of the bananas for a minute on each side.
Combine the sugar, orange juice, and rind. Pour over the bananas.
Simmer bananas and sauce over low heat for about 10 to 15 minutes or until bananas are tender.
Turn the bananas and spoon syrup over them while still cooking.
Serve warm with a sauce made by combining equal parts of sour cream and confectioner's sugar.
Serves 4.

Hint: To keep bananas fresh for longer periods, wrap each one in its peel in aluminum foil, and place it in the vegetable bin of your refrigerator. Remove the banana from the refrigerator for a few minutes before using. Bananas stored in this manner will keep for up to 3 weeks.

GINGER FLAN

This superb recipe comes from Liesel Flashenberg, Executive Director of Through the Kitchen Door. Make it for company and don't be left alone with any - you'll eat it all yourself!

1 cup sugar	1 cup heavy cream
1/3 cup water	1 1/ 4 cups sugar
2 Tablespoons light corn syrup	1/ 4 teaspoon salt
4 drops of lemon juice	3 Tablespoons chopped fresh ginger
2 vanilla beans, split lengthwise	4 whole eggs
3 cups milk	7 egg yolks

In a heavy saucepan over medium heat slowly stir the sugar, water, corn syrup and lemon juice until the sugar is dissolved. Let the mixture boil, carefully, until it turns caramel color (if it is not boiling fast enough it will not change color) then immediately remove from heat and pour into a 2 quart mold (or baking pan or individual molds). Swirl caramel around so it covers the bottom and set aside. Preheat oven to 350°F.
In a heavy saucepan, stirring occasionally, heat the seeds from the split vanilla beans, the milk, cream, sugar, and salt, stirring slowly. When mixture begins to boil, reduce heat and add the chopped fresh ginger. Simmer gently for about 5 minutes and then remove the mixture from the heat and let it cool, (but do not stir), about 15 to 20 minutes. Strain the milk and discard the ginger.

(continued on next page)

In a large bowl, using a whisk, gently beat together the eggs and egg yolks. Place a cup of the milk mixture in a small bowl, and slowly whisk in about 1/4 cup of the egg mixture. (The mixture should not curdle. If it does, discard it and let milk mixture cool more.) Whisk the egg/ milk mixture back into the milk mixture and whisk in remaining egg mixture.

Strain the flan mixture through a sieve into the prepared mold or pan. Place a kitchen towel in the bottom of a baking pan that is larger than the flan pan. Place the pan with the flan on the towel and carefully add enough boiling water to the pan (not into the pan with the flan) until it is about 1 1/2 inches deep. Bake for 1 hour or until a knife inserted into the center of the flan comes out clean. Carefully remove the flan from the oven and immediately place in the refrigerator to chill. When it is cold, cover with plastic wrap. It will stay about 4 days. Serve from the mold or loosen edges and turn out onto a serving plate. Serves 12.

HINT: Ginger is fresh when you can peel it with your finger nail...if it is this fresh you do not need to peel it for the recipe.

BLACK BOTTOM CUPCAKES

Filling:

8 ounces cream cheese, softened to room
   temperature
1 large egg, well beaten

1/3 cup sugar
pinch of salt
6 ounces semi sweet chocolate chips

Cake:

1 1/2 cups all purpose flour
1/3 cup sugar
1/4 cup unsweetened cocoa
1 teaspoon baking soda
pinch of salt

1 cup water
1/3 cup canola oil
1 Tablespoon vinegar
1 teaspoon vanilla

In a medium bowl, with an electric mixer at medium speed, beat the cream cheese with the egg, sugar, and salt until smooth. Stir in the chocolate chips and set aside.

Preheat the oven to 350°F. Place paper cupcake liners in 2" or 3" muffin tins.

In another bowl, sift together the flour, sugar, cocoa, baking soda, and salt.

Add the water, oil, vinegar, and vanilla, and mix well by hand.

Fill the cupcake liners halfway full with the cake batter.

Drop about 1 teaspoon of the cream cheese filling into the cake batter.

Bake for 20 minutes or until the cake part tests done.

Cool on a wire rack for 10 minutes before removing them from the tins.

Chill for several hours or overnight before serving, or else it will be difficult to peel the paper liners off of the cupcakes. These freeze beautifully in freezer baggies.

Makes 2 to 3 dozen.

BAKLAVA

This is "the real thing" and well worth the little bit of extra work required. Freezes beautifully.

approximately 2 cups melted butter or
   margarine (canola oil can be used)
1 pound phyllo dough, defrosted (if it was
   frozen), at room temperature
3 to 4 cups coarsely chopped almonds (not
   blanched) with skin if desired
1 cup sugar combined with 2 Tablespoons
   cinnamon

3 cups sugar
1 1/2 cups water
juice of 1/2 lemon
grated rind of 1 lemon
grated rind of 1 orange
1 cinnamon stick

Preheat the oven to 350°F.

Grease the bottom and sides of a 9" x 13" baking pan with some of the melted butter.

Place one sheet of phyllo into the pan and brush thoroughly with melted butter, then lay another sheet of phyllo on top, brush with butter, and repeat the process until you have used 5 sheets.

Sprinkle the 5th sheet with about 3 TBL of the chopped almonds and 1 TBL of the sugar/cinnamon mixture. Then place another sheet of phyllo on top, and brush with melted butter.

Place another sheet of phyllo on top, and sprinkle with about 3 TBL nuts and sugar mixture.

Repeat the procedure, spreading the phyllo sheets alternately with the nuts and sugar, then the melted butter until you have only 5 phyllo sheets left.

The last 5 sheets should be brushed with melted butter, but leave the top sheet dry (no butter) and sprinkle it with cold water.

Bake the baklava for 45 minutes. Remove the pan from the oven and cool slightly on a wire rack.

With a sharp knife, cut diagonally 2/3rds of the way through the baklava (but not to the bottom), first in one direction, then in the other to form diamond shaped pieces.

In a large pot, combine the sugar, water, lemon juice, lemon rind, orange rind, and the cinnamon stick to make the syrup.

Bring mixture to a boil, reduce heat, and cook, stirring for about 10 minutes. Remove from heat and let the syrup cool, removing the cinnamon stick.

Pour syrup over the baklava and chill for an hour or more, and just before serving finish cutting the diamonds all the way down to the bottom so the pieces can be easily removed from the pan.

Makes about 2 1/2 dozen pieces.

HINT: When measuring honey or any other sticky substances, grease the measuring cup first.

CAROL ERLICH'S CHOCOLATE BREAD PUDDING

2 cups milk
8 ounces semi sweet chocolate
4 ounces butter
1/2 cup sugar

3 large eggs, lightly beaten
2 teaspoons vanilla
6 slices white, crustless bread cut in 1/2" cubes

Preheat oven to 350°F.
In a pot over medium heat, heat the milk, chocolate, butter, and sugar, stirring until melted.
Remove from the heat and beat with a whisk until smooth and warm enough to put your finger in.
Add the beaten eggs and vanilla, mixing well.
Stir in the bread and pour into a lightly greased 1 1/2 quart baking pan, or 9"x13" cake pan.
Place the baking pan in a larger pan (water bath) filled with 1" of boiling water.
Bake for 45 minutes or until a knife inserted in the center comes out clean.
Serves 8.

HEAVENLY FRUIT MELANGE

The ultimate dessert to serve at extra large, extra special gatherings. I call it "The Happy Dessert" because eating it makes me very very happy!!!

12 naval oranges, peeled, sectioned, and
coarsely chopped
4 cans (16 ounces each) pitted black cherries,
drained
2 cans (20 ounces each) sliced peaches, drained
4 cans (15 ounces each) pineapple chunks,
drained

8 bananas, sliced
1 1/2 to 2 cups orange liqueur
1/2 gallon vanilla ice cream, slightly softened
1 pint orange sherbet, slightly softened
2 jars (12 ounce each) orange marmalade

Place the pieces of orange on the bottom of a very large punch bowl.
Place the drained cherries on top the oranges, then a layer of peaches, pineapple chunks, and finally the sliced bananas. Cover the mixture with 3/4 to 1 cup of the liqueur, cover the bowl with foil and let the mixture sit at room temperature for as long as possible (an hour or two or all day).
One hour before serving, spread the vanilla ice cream in pieces about an inch thick over the top of the fruit. Spread the orange sherbet on top of the ice cream, like icing.
Heat the marmalade with the remaining liqueur in a small pan.
Bring to a boil, reduce heat to simmer, and stir and cook for another minute or two, mixing well.
Spread this hot mixture over the sherbet layer. Do not mix anything yet.
Refrigerate the dessert (or let it sit out) for about an hour.
Toss everything together from the bottom up and serve. (I serve it with a variety of cookies.)
Serves 35 or more.

HORATIO'S VELVET CHOCOLATE MOUSSE

You can make this ahead, but there will not be any left for your company! I found this unique mousse in Hawaii. After eating 3 bowls full I begged the owner of the restaurant for the recipe.

12 ounces cream cheese, at room temperature   1/4 cup unsweetened cocoa
1 to 1 1/2 cups sugar   1 cup whipping cream
1 1/2 teaspoons vanilla

In a mixing bowl, with an electric mixer at medium speed, beat the cream cheese, sugar and the vanilla until very light and fluffy - about 10 minutes, making sure sugar is well dissolved. If texture is grainy when you taste it, then beat longer. Add the cocoa and beat until the mixture is smooth and the cocoa is dissolved.
In another mixing bowl, with an electric mixer at high speed, whip the cream until soft peaks form. (If you over beat the cream, you will get butter!)
Fold the whipped cream into the cheese mixture one half at a time, using a rubber spatula.
Divide the mixture into individual dessert dishes or glasses or spoon it into a large serving bowl. Cover and refrigerate for at least 8 hours.
Serves 10 to 12.

IRRESISTIBLE CINNAMON BALLS

1 1/2 cups ground almonds   1 tablespoon cinnamon
1/3 cup superfine sugar   2 large egg whites, beaten until soft peaks form

In a bowl combine almonds, sugar, cinnamon, mixing well. Fold in beaten whites. Wet hands and form in small balls (about the size of a walnut) and place on a lined cookie sheet.
Preheat oven to 350°F.
Bake about 14 minutes, balls should be soft inside. If desired, dust with confectioners' sugar.
Makes about 16 balls.

"JUST ONE MORE" APRICOT BALLS FROM KITCHEN AFFAIRS

1 1/2 cups finely chopped dried apricots   2/3 cup condensed milk
2 cups shredded coconut   confectioners' sugar

In a medium size bowl, combine the chopped apricots, coconut, and milk. Roll into small balls, and roll the balls in confectioners' sugar. Place on a serving platter and chill, covered. Makes about 24 pieces.

LEMON CREAM CREPES

Crepes:

1 1/2 cups milk
3 large eggs
1 1/2 cups all purpose flour
1 Tablespoons sugar

1 teaspoon melted butter or margarine, cooled
2 Tablespoons melted butter or margarine for
    making crepes
superfine granulated sugar for baking crepes

Lemon Cream:

2 large eggs
1 large egg yoke
2/3 cup sugar

zest of one whole lemon
juice of one whole lemon
4 ounces butter or margarine

Place the milk, eggs, flour, sugar and cooled melted butter into a blend or processor and blend until smooth. If possible, let the batter sit at room temperature for 2 hours.

Heat a 6" or 7" crepe pan on medium heat for 3 to 4 minutes then brush lightly with melted butter or margarine, and let heat a minute.

Add just enough batter to barely cover the bottom of the crepe pan

Brown crepe lightly on one side, turn over and cook another minute.

Remove crepe from pan and repeat process, buttering pan as needed.

Stack crepes and cover with foil until serving time.

Makes about 20 crepes.

To prepare the lemon cream, beat the whole eggs and extra yolk together, and gradually add the sugar and beat to blend. Add the grated zest of the lemon and the lemon juice.

Add the butter and beat well. Place cream mixture in a heavy saucepan and cook, stirring constantly, over low heat until the mixture thickens and coats a wooden spoon. Do not let the mixture boil. If you want, this can be done in a double boiler.

When cream is thick, pour mixture into a bowl and place the bowl in another bowl filled with ice or ice water to cool quickly and prevent overcooking. Stir occasionally.

Refrigerate in a covered bowl or jar until ready for use. This makes about 1 1/2 cups.

Preheat oven to 300°F.

To serve, spread each crepe with a generous spoonful of lemon cream and roll like a cigarette. Place crepes close together in an ovenproof pan and sprinkle the tops generously with superfine granulated sugar. Dessert may be made ahead or the day before serving up to this point, covered with plastic wrap and refrigerated. Bake for 10 to 12 minutes.

Serves 6.

HINT: Batter should rest in the refrigerator for two hours. This allows for the flour particles to expand in the liquid and facilitates the dissipation of air bubbles. Both of these processes create a lighter, thinner, and tender batter. If the batter thickens upon resting, add a little water until the desired consistency is achieved.

NAPOLEONS CREME BRULEE

2 or 3 sheets puff pastry, defrosted, at
  room temperature

melted butter
light brown sugar

1 1/2 cups whipping cream
1 vanilla bean, - split lengthwise
9 large egg yolks

1/2 cup + 6 teaspoons sugar
2 tablespoons packed light brown sugar

On a lightly floured surface, roll out puff pastry. Cut into strips vertically, then into squares, and cut squares diagonally across to form triangles. Brush with melted butter and pat on gently the light brown sugar. Each sheet makes about 20 triangles. Bake at 375° to 400°F. Cool and store until ready to serve with creme brulee.

Heat oven to 325°F. Place cream in heavy medium saucepan. Scrape in seeds from vanilla bean; add bean. Bring to simmer over medium heat. Whisk yolks and 1/2 cup sugar in medium metal bowl to blend. Set bowl over saucepan of simmering water (do not allow bowl to touch water). Whisk vigorously until yolk mixture is pale yellow and hot to touch, about 3 minutes. Gradually whisk in hot cream mixture; discard vanilla bean.
To make Napoleons, bake custard in 13" x 9" glass pan, set inside a larger pan filled with enough hot water to come halfway up the sides of the glass pan. Bake custard 45 to 50 minutes. Should be firm with a wiggle like set Jello. Refrigerator overnight. To assemble: Place one triangle on plate, spoon (or pipe) with creme brulee, angle other triangle on top. Serve with strawberries or other fruit. Serves 1

PEARS ALI BABA

The perfect finale to eat after an elaborate dinner.

6 to 8 firm fresh pears
3 cups dry white wine
1/2 cup sugar
2" piece of vanilla bean
2 cups fresh strawberries

2 cups fresh raspberries or 12 ounce box of
   frozen raspberries, thawed and drained
3 cups whipping cream
1/2 cup sifted confectioner's sugar
1/3 cup red port wine (approximately)

Several hours or the day before serving, carefully peel the pears, keeping the surface as smooth as possible, leaving the stems on.
In a large skillet, gently heat the wine and stirring with a whisk, dissolve the sugar in it.
Lay the pears in the sweetened wine, add the vanilla bean, and bring the wine to a boil.
Reduce the heat and poach the fruit until it is tender but still firm, about 15 to 20 minutes.
Remove the skillet from the heat and allow the pears to cool in the wine mixture.
Chill the pears in the poaching liquid until ice cold.
Wash and hull the strawberries and press them through a sieve with a wooden spoon.
Crush the raspberries and force them through a sieve to remove all the seeds.
Mix the two fruit purees together and chill them - the mixture should be very cold and thick enough to "mask" the pears.
In a large bowl, with the electric mixer on high, whip two of the cups of cream until soft peaks form. Add the confectioner's sugar and continue beating until the cream is very firm and stiff.
Fold in the port wine, using only as much as the cream will hold without becoming too soft or liquid. Chill the mixture.
In another bowl, with the mixer at high speed, whip the remaining cup of cream until stiff peaks form and chill it. This cream is to be used for decoration if desired.
To assemble the dessert, cover the bottom of a round, shallow serving dish with the port-flavored whipping cream and arrange the pears carefully on top.
Spoon the fruit puree carefully over each pear, masking the entire surface.
Spoon any remaining puree around the base of the pears to cover the whipped cream.
Decorate the base of the pears with the plain whipped cream, using a pastry bag with a star tip.
Serves 6 to 8.

SOUTHWEST BREAD PUDDING WITH TEQUILA SAUCE

On my first trip to Santa Fe, I ate at a well-known restaurant. This is an adaptation of their fabulous bread pudding.

1/2 pound stale French bread	1 1/4 cups sugar
1 cup milk	1/4 cup dark brown sugar
1/4 pound (1 stick) butter, melted	4 ounce can skim evaporated milk
1/2 cup golden raisins	8 1/4 ounce can crushed pineapple with juice
1/3 cup pine nuts	1 teaspoon fresh lemon juice
3 large eggs, beaten or an egg substitute	3 teaspoons vanilla

Tequila Sauce:

1 cup granulated sugar	1/3 cup good quality tequila without the worm
1 large egg	1 teaspoon lime juice
1/4 pound butter, melted	

Preheat the oven to 350°F.
Break bread into bite size chunks, place in a large bowl. Pour in the milk and soak the bread.
Squeeze the bread with your fingers to eliminate excess liquid and discard milk.
Add remaining ingredients, except those for the sauce, to the wet bread.
Very gently, mix thoroughly. Pour mixture into an 9" x 13" buttered baking pan.
Bake for an hour or until a knife inserted in the center comes out clean.
Serve with sauce.
To prepare sauce: cream sugar and egg together, then add the butter and pour into a medium saucepan. Cook, stirring over a low flame until sugar is dissolved. Remove from heat and stir in tequila and lime juice. Pour over servings of bread pudding.
Serves 10 to 12.

NOTE: if serving this with rum sauce instead of Tequila Sauce, eliminate lime juice and substitute rum. This can be made "low fat" by substituting egg beaters, a lite butter, skim evaporated milk, and 1/4 cup less sugar.

STRAWBERRIES WITH AMARETTO SAUCE

This is the kind of dessert where you would lick the plate if you thought no one was looking!

3 cups fresh strawberries, cleaned and hulled
4 Tablespoons Amaretto liqueur
4 Tablespoons confectioner's sugar
8 ounces cream cheese, softened to room
  temperature

8 ounces sour cream
1/2 cup sugar
4 large egg yolks*
4 Tablespoons Amaretto liqueur
2 Tablespoons whipping cream

Toss the berries in a large bowl with the Amaretto and the confectioner's sugar. Set aside to chill.
In a blender or food processor, mix together the remaining ingredients.
Blend until smooth, but if using the food processor use quick on and off turns until sauce is
smooth. Pour sauce into a bowl and refrigerate until well chilled.
Place berries in wineglasses or a large bowl and top with sauce and serve.
Serves 6 to 8.

*When a recipe calls for egg yolks (raw) place the yolks and a tablespoon of water or liquid for
each yolk in a pot over low heat, and slowly whisk until mixture is thick enough to coat a wooden
spoon (160F). Place pot in a bowl with ice and cool mixture, then proceed to use as recipe directs.

SHORT CUT FUDGE

This is Nancy Baggett's famous fudge. She is the author of *THE ALL AMERICAN COOKIE BOOK*,
and a well known authority on American sweets.

14 ounce can sweetened condensed milk
2 Tablespoon unsalted butter, cut into pieces
12 ounces semisweet chocolate chips
2 ounces unsweetened chocolate, finely chopped
1 teaspoon vanilla

2 to 3 cups mini marshmallows
1 cup dried sweetened cranberries – opt.
4 ounces chopped pecans or walnuts,
  optional

Line an 8" sq. pan with foil, extending 2" over the sides. Spray generously with oil.
Heat the milk and butter in medium pan over medium-low heat, stirring almost constantly, just until
butter melts. Do not scorch mixture. Add chocolate chips, chopped chocolate, reduce heat to low
and heat, stirring constantly, until chocolate melts. Immediately remove from the heat, add vanilla,
and stir until completely mixed. Add the marshmallows, berries, nuts, mix well. Scrape fudge into
pan. Press smooth with an oiled knife. Cool on a wire rack to room temperature. Refrigerate for at
least 1 hour prior to cutting. Remove fudge by pulling out foil. Invert and cut. Pack in airtight tins
with wax paper between layers and refrigerate.

WHITE CHOCOLATE SUNDRIED CHERRY BREAD PUDDING

Another one of Phyllis Frucht's great recipes.

1 cup sundried cherries
1/3 cup Kirsch
4 cups Italian or French bread, cubed
3/4 cup sugar
1 pint milk

1 pint heavy cream
1 stick unsweetened butter, melted
4 large eggs
1/2 pound white chocolate chunks
1 teaspoon vanilla

Preheat the oven to 400°F.

Combine the cherries and Kirsch in a small bowl and let stand until plumped, about an hour, mixing occasionally.

Combine the bread, sugar, milk, cream, melted butter, and eggs in a large bowl and let stand for an hour. Mash well with a fork and add the vanilla, berries, Kirsch, and chocolate chunks.

Pour into a well buttered shallow 2 1/2 to 3 quart ovenproof bowl, smooth the top and bake for 40 minutes or until a knife inserted comes out clean.

Serve warm or chilled or with Raspberry Coulis, or whipped cream if desired. Garnish with fresh raspberries.

RASPBERRY COULIS

1 package frozen raspberries in heavy syrup, thawed

1 tablespoon lemon juice
1 tablespoon kirsch

In processor or blender, puree the ingredients until smooth then strain to remove seeds.
Serves 8.

TRES LECHE

I looked long and hard for the best Tres Leche cake recipe I could find. There were all kinds of versions, but the best was from Nestle and I found it in my CHOW newsletter (Culinary Historians of Washington). Tres Leche means Cake with Three Milks. It is just decadent.

Cake:

6 large eggs divided into whites and yolks
1/2 cup sugar, divided

1 cup all purpose flour, sifted

Cream:

14 ounce can sweetened condensed milk
1 cup table cream
5 ounce can evaporated milk

1/4 cup dark rum
1 teaspoon vanilla

Topping:

1 cup whipping cream
2 tablespoons sugar

1/2 teaspoon vanilla

Garnish: coconut, toasted slivered almonds - optional

Preheat oven to 375°F. Grease and flour a 9" springform pan.
In a mixer, using a whisk beater if possible, beat whites and 1/4 cup sugar until stiff peaks form.
In another bowl, beat 1/4 cup sugar and yolks for 5 to 8 minutes or until light and lemon colored.
Carefully fold the whites, alternating with the flour, into the beaten yolks. Pour into the prepared pan and bake for 15 to 20 minutes or until a toothpick inserted in the center of the cake comes out clean. Remove pan and place on a wire rack and let cool for 20 minutes.
Carefully remove the cake from the pan and place in a 1" deep serving dish, like a porcelain quiche pan.
Prepare cream by mixing together the condensed milk, whipping cream, evaporated milk, rum, and vanilla. Mix well. Prick all over the top of the cake with a fork, and slowly pour the cream over the top of the cake, letting the cream soak into the holes. Spoon any excess cream from the serving dish back onto the top of the cake. Let cake sit for 30 minutes or until it absorbs as much of the cream as possible.

Topping:
Beat the cream, sugar, and vanilla in a small mixer bowl until stiff peaks form. Spread evenly over the top of the cake and the sides of the cake. Serve immediately with any remaining cream. Can also garnish with coconut and toasted slivered almond. Serves 8.

ITALIAN RUM CAKE

Save this for a very special occasion as it is very rich and requires a good deal of advance preparation.

Cake:

7 large eggs, separated	1 tablespoon grated lemon zest
1 cup confectioners' sugar	1 tablespoon sweet vermouth
1 cup sifted cake flour	

Preheat oven to 350F. Butter (and dust with flour) 2 8-inch round cake pans with confectioners' sugar. Using a mixer, beat the yolks and sugar at high speed until lemon colored (about 3 to 5 minutes). Reduce mixer to the lowest speed and add flour, zest, and vermouth. Beat just until flour is incorporated.

In a separate bowl, using a whip beater, beat the whites until they hold a peak. Fold 1/3 of the whites into the yolk mixture, then fold in the remaining beaten whites. Pour into the prepared cake pans and bake 25 to 30 minutes. Cool 10 minutes and remove from pans. Let cool.

Rum Syrup:

1 1/4 cup sugar	2 lemon slices
4 orange slices	2/3 cup golden rum

In a small pan combine sugar, 1 cup water, and fruit slices. Bring to boil stirring constantly. Boil gently uncovered, for 20 minutes. Discard fruit and stir in the rum.
Set aside until cool.

Cheese Filling and Topping:

1 lb ricotta cheese	4 oz mixed candied fruits, finely
1/2 cup confectioners' sugar plus 2 tablespoons	chopped
	1 tablespoon rum
1/2 cup semisweet chocolate morsels	about 1/3 cup seedless raspberry jam
2 tablespoons melted semisweet chocolate morsels	1 cup heavy cream

In a bowl combine 1 cup of ricotta cheese, 1/2 cup confectioners' sugar and beat for about 3 minutes. Stir in 1/2 cup of semisweet chocolate morsels, candied fruits, and rum. Mix well.

In another small bowl combine 1 cup of ricotta cheese and the melted chocolate morsels until blended. Refrigerate fillings until ready to assemble the cake.

To assemble the cake: Split each cake into two layers. Place a layer, cut side up, on a plate. Drizzle with 1/2 cup of the rum syrup. Spread with half of the plain cheese filling. Spread

(continued on next page)

cut side down layer with 1 / 2 of the raspberry jam. Place jam side down over cheese layer, and drizzle top of cake with 1/ 2 cup of rum syrup.

Spread the top of the cake with all of the chocolate cheese filling. Add third layer, cut side up. Spread with rest of plain cheese filling. Spread remaining jam over cut side of fourth layer and place jam side down over cheese layer. Drizzle with remaining syrup.

Beat the cream and 2 tablespoons of confectioners' sugar until stiff. Frost top and sides of cake. Refrigerate overnight until serving.

Serves 10 generously.

MOLTEN CHOCOLATE LAVA COOKIES

A friend gave me this recipe a few years ago, and now I make it for every occasion. They freeze beautifully. Just defrost and reheat in the microwave.

4 cups (24 oz.) semisweet chocolate
  chips
6 tablespoons butter
4 large eggs
1 cup sugar

1 teaspoon salt (I used less)
2 teaspoons vanilla
2 cups all purpose flour
1 teaspoon baking powder

Melt chips and butter in top of double boiler over low heat, stirring until smooth but thick. Remove from heat; set aside to cool.

In large bowl of mixer beat eggs, sugar, salt and vanilla on high speed about 2 to 3 minutes until pale yellow and slightly thickened. Mix in chocolate on low speed. Stop and scrape bowl. Add flour and baking powder on low speed just until incorporated, stopping once to scrape bowl. Cover dough with plastic wrap and refrigerate for 15 to 30 minutes. Don't let dough get too hard.

Preheat oven to 375°F. Scoop eight 1 to 1 1/ 2-inch mounds onto parchment lined cookie sheet, leaving 2" between cookies. Bake one sheet at a time for 12 minutes or until crusty on the outside but soft in the center. Cool on cookie sheet 3 to 5 minutes. Best when served warm. To reheat cookies so the centers become soft again, microwave on high power for about 10 seconds per cookie (low wattage microwaves may require an additional 5 seconds per cookie).

Makes about 30 cookies.

DOUBLE CHOCOLATE CHOCOLATE CHIP COOKIES

This recipe by Chaim Potter won the best chocolate chip cookie award from Copia: Amererican Center for Wine, Food & Arts, Napa, Ca. I friend sent it to me knowing my addiction to fabulous chocolate cookies.

1 cup flour
1/ 2 cup unsweetened Dutch process
  cocoa power
1 teaspoon ground cinnamon
1/ 2 teaspoon baking soda
1/ 2 teaspoon kosher salt
1/ 8 teaspoon finely ground black pepper

1/ 4 lb. coarsely chopped good quality dark
  bittersweet chocolate
1/ 2 cup unsalted butter
1 1/ 2 cups sugar
2 large eggs
1 teaspoon vanilla
3/ 4 cup semisweet chocolate chips

Preheat oven to 325F. Line 17x12-inch cook sheet with parchment
In a small bowl, whisk together flour, cocoa, cinnamon, baking soda, salt, and pepper. Set a side. Carefully, in the microwave melt chocolate with butter over high heat for one minute, remove and stir to finish melting, or heat again for about 20 seconds and stir well to finish melting. Let cool slightly.
With your mixer on medium speed, mix melted chocolate with sugar, eggs, and vanilla until combined. Reduce speed to low and gradually add flour. Fold in the chips.
Using a 1 1/ 2-inch ice cream scoop, drop scoops of dough 2-inches apart on prepared pan. Bake about 15 minutes until cookies are soft, look flat, and surface cracks. Let cool in pan on wire cooling rack. Store at room temperature for 3 days.
Makes about 36.

INDEX

A

D

FRUIT

K

L

M

N

P

Simply Irresistible
Easy, Elegant, Fearless, Fussless, Recipes
Sheilah Kaufman
10508 Tyler Terrace
Potomac, MD 20854

e-mail: www.cookingwithsheilah.com

Please send me _____ copies of your cookbook at $17.95 per copy plus $3.25 per copy for postage and handling. Enclosed is my check or money order for $ _____ .

Name: _____

Address: _____

City, State, Zip: _____

✂ — ✂

Simply Irresistible
Easy, Elegant, Fearless, Fussless, Recipes
Sheilah Kaufman
10508 Tyler Terrace
Potomac, MD 20854

e-mail: www.cookingwithsheilah.com

Please send me _____ copies of your cookbook at $17.95 per copy plus $3.25 per copy for postage and handling. Enclosed is my check or money order for $ _____ .

Name: _____

Address: _____

City, State, Zip: _____